The Leader's Guide

To Change Management

By

Lawrence M. Miller
&
Helene F. Uhlfelder

Miller/Howard Consulting Group, Inc.
Atlanta, Georgia
Copyright, 1997

Published by Miller/Howard Publishers, Inc.
750 Hammond Drive
Building 12, Suite 200
Atlanta, Georgia 30328
(404) 255-6523
http://www.millerhoward.com

ISBN: 0-9629679-7-1

Table of Contents

Preface & Acknowledgement

One of the joys of management consulting is the opportunity to learn, to explore ideas, experiment, and hopefully, discover better ways to improve organizations. We have never found the one best way to design or manage an organization. Humility may be the first and most important virtue of one who seeks to help others. We hope we display this in our work because it is the essential antecedent to learning.

As we have experimented and improved our methods we have revised our materials. The accompanying workbook on *Change Management* is the third or fourth evolution of our guide to process and organization redesign. Unfortunately, it has grown in thickness. During the last revision we realized that many leaders of organizations would not take the time to go through all of the detailed techniques of managing change, and didn't need to. It is for this reason that we decided to pull out the essentials and include the key messages for those leading change in this Leader's Guide. We hope it serves the purpose of guiding leaders to those critical actions that will assure the success of their improvement efforts.

Virtually every useful method in the workbook and this Leader's Guide are the result of our field experience. We have been enormously blessed to work with some of the finest companies and people in the corporate world. Without their openness, effort, and feedback we would have little to offer to others. We can only say the most sincere thank you for helping us in our efforts to improve our methods and to help others.

The writing of Part One of this guide is the work of both authors and is a condensed version of the workbook. Part Two is the writing of the first author.

No one has been more essential to the production of both of these books than Karen Slot, Michelle Tisdale, and Claudia Kilgore who have corrected thousands of examples of misplaced commas and poor grammar. They have also displayed the utmost patience and tolerance of the author's tendency to chaos and lack of discipline. Many of our consultants have also contributed both to the editing and to the substance of the material in these works. We would especially like to thank Jennifer Howard, Will Jones, Tom Akins, John Burden, Duane Cross, Chris Head, Jack Hinzman, Carol Phillips, Russ Ridley, Ron Robinson, and Susan Shaw.

Introduction

This *Leader's Guide to Change Management* is a companion book to *Change Management: Creating the Dynamic Organization Through Whole System Architecture.* The purpose of this book is direct and simple. All of the techniques, methods, and change processes described in the accompanying workbook, or any other source, amount to less than fifty percent of that which is required to create significant change in the culture and performance of an organization. The other fifty percent is you! Leaders change organizations, not techniques. We have redesigned more than one hundred organizations and the single most obvious fact of change management is that change is successful when the leadership and the leadership team are willing to personally engage in the struggle. Leader's and leadership teams must be willing to change their own method of operation, their own style, behavior, and priorities. The purpose of this book is to help you redefine your own role, to help you lead change.

Prepare to struggle!

We will discuss many keys to successful change management in this book. However, there are a few thoughts that may be at the heart of your success as a change leader.

1. Create Alignment of the Whole System

In the frantic rush to gain competitive advantage, companies initiated multiple programs, processes, and practices. Because many of these efforts died midstream or did not produce results, people are cynical. At one point in 1997 two of the top ten management books were based on cartoons written by Scott Adams, the creator of Dilbert and Dogbert. The plethora of tools, techniques, gurus, models, and processes available spawned an industry that pokes fun at them all. To employees, many efforts appear to be superficial, disjointed, and independent of real value adding work or bottom line results.

Managers and management have become overly specialized and fragmented. People identify with a particular function such as finance, production, sales, or human resources. Every function has different scorecards, language, and systems. The systems do not fit together and often conflict. With increasingly narrow expertise and specialization, the average employee or manager no longer understands the business. When employees do not feel responsible for the business, companies do not do well. Organizations do well when employees are engaged and actively pursue the success of the business as a whole.

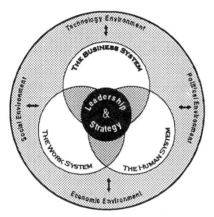

Successful change management and successful business management require effective integration and alignment of systems and structure to support an effective culture. It requires concurrent attention to all of the major elements that impact organizational performance. This requires understanding that the organization is a system and consciously designing the system to achieve business results.

To do this we propose a simple model that shows the integration and interconnection of the organization's system and three major subsystems. This model shows how leadership and business strategy impact the system and its results. The model illustrates the overlap or interaction of the subsystems. Change one, and it necessarily impacts the others.

Effective change management is the result of creating alignment of these systems to each other and to the requirements of the environment and business strategy. The number one cause of failure of reengineering, TQM, or other change efforts has been the failure to understand *"whole systems,"* or complexity, the interdependence of the systems. Too many companies and leaders are still relying on the mental models of Henry Ford's factory, dealing separately with each component and delegating responsibility for the parts. Strategy is dealt with separately from work processes and their capabilities. Human competencies are not considered in strategy or work process redesign. And, employee involvement and other "people programs" are isolated from the business scorecard and strategy. Each of these separations is a mental breakdown that causes failure in change management.

2. Moving Toward a Company of Business Managers

Over the last twenty years there has been increased appreciation of the benefits organizations can reap from involving employees in all aspects of managing the business. How organizations use employee involvement ranges from task teams recommending dress codes to teams managing their budgets, hiring team members, and being responsible for bottom line financial measures. Employee involvement is moving from partial involvement in fixing immediate partners to a new organizational system in which employees increasingly accept responsibility as partners in business management.

Can all managers and all employees become business managers? Yes. It is not that hard. Family farmers are business managers. Store-owners are business managers. Artisans for generations have been business managers. Why can't a vice president of technology, a sales manager, or an employee in a research lab or an auto plant be a business manager? They can if they are given necessary information, involved in the process, asked the right questions, and allowed to make decisions that have an impact. It is the nature of the system that has denied employees the tools to be involved in business management. When every employee is a student of the numbers and is constantly seeking to improve the numbers, you have a system that produces high performance.

To be a business manager is to understand and feel responsible for the whole organization: for the owners, customers, employees, and all of the pieces that fit together to produce business performance. A business manager is in touch with the real numbers that are the measure of business performance. These are the numbers that owners care about most. They are the numbers that investors understand and which cause the value of the company's stock to increase or decrease. For too long we have assumed that only the senior managers, financial managers, or business unit managers were capable of managing to these numbers. We know that this is no longer true. We know how to create a system, in small and large organizations, where every employee feels the connection to business performance felt by a small business owner.

3. Perseverance: Staying on Course

Significant change often occurs in wave patterns. You can see this wave pattern in the adoption of total quality management, employee involvement, lean production, and reengineering. First, corporations discover a new methodology. The new method is met with skepticism and disbelief. A few committed true believers emerge who promote it from within the organization. External gurus write books and give motivational speeches. Conferences are held, and new associations formed. Gradually, as success stories are promoted, more companies and managers buy-in. The new technique becomes something everyone is doing. Social pressure requires at least the appearance of adopting the new method. With buy-in, a critical stage is reached. Some organizations will say they have "done it" if they have talked about it and trained some people. They will go on to search for the next new technique before they have ever consolidated or mastered the old one. They fall off the wave just as it is at its crest.

Some organizations go on to consolidate the new process within the company so that it becomes a normal way of life. They ride the wave onto the shore. These companies integrate the new method into their systems and structure, assuring its continuance and the development of competence. They demonstrate and value the new methods throughout the organization, hold all employees accountable for competence and performance, and reap rewards in the form of higher productivity and quality.

More companies fail to develop competence and maintain the change than actually develop competence. They abandon the technique in its "program" stage assuring the organization's behavior will revert to previous norms. They spend a lot of money but do not see a return on the investment. This produces skepticism, which makes it even harder for the organization to climb the next wave.

Adopting a new management methodology, including whole system architecture, the redesign of the organization's systems and structure for business results, is not enough. The redesigned organization must stay on the wave all the way through to competence to harvest the benefits of the new system. This workbook will cover why and how to stay on course through implementation and continuing improvement.

4. A Unified Change Management Process

Problems and solutions begin in the mind. How the mind works is conditioned by cultural history. The mind of most managers today is the product of a hundred years of organizations built on the models of manufacturing management derived from Henry Ford and Frederick Taylor. To manufacture cars efficiently, you create a separate engine design and manufacturing group, a separate body group, and the same for electronics, and other components. Homebuilders subcontract with specialists who concern themselves only with the foundation, roofing, electrical, or plumbing. We have learned to solve problems by dividing them into pieces and delegating responsibility for each piece to a separate individual or group. For many problems this works well. To change a complex and interdependent system, a culture, an economy, or an organization, it leads to failure.

Modern manufacturing seeks to create continuous flow, seamless processes and the elimination of walls such as those traditionally found between design, engineering and manufacturing. Similarly, the best change processes are a continuous flow, a seamless process that incorporates strategy, business requirements, work processes, and human systems. Whole System Architecture is to change management what lean production is to manufacturing. It is an understanding of the unity of the system and a process for reconsidering the system as an organic whole. This has proven to produce results faster, with less rework, frustration and more permanent change.

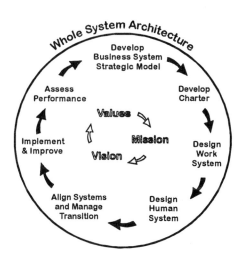

Whole System Architecture creates an internal capability for adaptation. We live in a constantly changing environment. Changes in the systems and structure of the organization will be continuous for the remainder of our careers. It is a goal of this book to help you create the internal competence to manage changes more effectively on an ongoing basis.

Chapter One

Whole System Architecture:
Principles & Process

Most skilled physicians recognize the interdependence of the systems that comprise the human body. A headache may not be an indication of something wrong with the brain, but of stress or dietary problems. A fever may be caused by problems in any one of a dozen subsystems of the body. Similarly, the performance of a company may be the result of a series of interactions between different subsystems of the organization. Low sales may be an indicator of poor product quality or design, not merely a failure of the sales process. A failure of manufacturing performance may result from inadequate supply chain information. This may be the result of poor hiring and training or poor computers and software.

Despite the obvious interrelationship of corporate systems, most change efforts are trapped by the divide and conquer mentality of solving problems. The most common traps of change management are the following:

1. The Cost Cutting Trap: This trap occurs when the focus is only on the business system, and the work process and human systems are ignored. The organization can be led into this trap by leaders who have lost patience with efforts to improve financial performance by other means. Cutting expenses often appears to be the only solution. Of course, there are times when cutting expenses is necessary. A continuous series of cost reduction efforts, however, inevitably reduces the capability of the organization to create new products, services and revenue. If there had been a focus on improving capabilities in response to market requirements the downward spiral of cost cutting can be avoided. This is a failure of strategy. The cost cutting trap usually indicates that the organization has failed to:

- Focus on root causes of poor revenue growth.
- Listen to customers and improve quality.
- Build and invest in new capabilities.
- Study and continuously improve processes.

- Align human resources properly.
- Share financial data and include employees in managing the business.

2. The People Focus Trap: This happens when the focus is on the human system, and the business and work systems are ignored. The nicest people in the organization can fall into this trap. They believe that making people happy or just providing more training will improve business performance. This is sometimes true, but rarely. You can have happy, well trained people making buggy whips and still go out of business. You can give everyone team-building experiences and have teams working in poorly designed processes and not improve their numbers. The people focus trap usually indicates the organization has failed to:

- Focus everyone on the real competitive situation and the business facts.
- Align training and development to business needs.
- Focus on satisfy financial stakeholders.
- Optimize utilization of assets.
- Analyze and improve work processes.
- Employ technology solutions.

3. The Process Focus Trap: This happens when the focus is only on the work system and omits the human and business systems. This may also be called the reengineering trap. Most organizations have learned that great improvements can be made by studying and improving work processes. Company after company has also learned that the best designed process fails to be implemented if the organization of people, their skills, incentives, and accountability do not change along with the process. Several studies found that the majority of reengineering projects failed to improve business performance. The primary reason was the failure to change the culture, the human systems, and human behavior. Also, many reengineering or process improvement projects start out without any direct linkage to business performance or business strategy. The process improvement trap usually indicates the organization has failed to:

- Help people understand the business strategy.
- Give employees critical business information and involve them in managing their performance.
- Redesign and modify human systems to support the redesigned processes.
- Build revenue through new capabilities.

- Consider how all processes impact each other and how changing one process may cause problems in others.

Most companies have fallen into one of these traps. The three subsystems of the organization are designed and managed by different people based on different principles to achieve different goals. This is the low alignment organization. Alignment of the three subsystems is associated with high performance. An organization in which all three subsystems are designed to support the strategy and each other has the highest likelihood of satisfying customers and shareholders.

Whole System Architecture Defined

Whole System Architecture (WSA) avoids the pitfalls of single system solutions and addresses the reality of the organization's complexity and interdependence. *Whole System Architecture is the process of analyzing all internal and external factors that affect organization performance then designing the organization's systems and creating alignment among those systems based on defined principles and business strategy.*

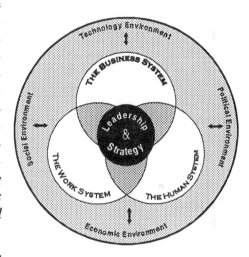

Whole System Architecture begins with a study of the environment that influences and creates requirements for the organization. This study will include customer requirements, market trends, technology trends, social changes, and potential changes in the economy. The business system includes both strategic positioning and financial performance. Too many change programs fail to begin with the end in mind, the actual business performance that will meet both shareholder requirements and create capital for future expansion. The work processes are defined and redesigned based on an analysis of the capabilities required to perform consistent with the strategy. The human system includes everything regarding people, their hiring, competencies, motivation, organization, and communication. Clearly, each of these must be designed in a manner that is consistent, and based on the same goals and requirements.

Whole System Architecture is an interactive planning process. The interaction begins with clear communication from the senior managers of the organization, the steering team. The purpose, underlying principles, strategy, boundaries, and objectives of the process are clearly spelled out in the *Charter*. The design charter is the formal statement of the leadership direction, their vision of the future. This charter is given to an appointed design team, or teams, that redesign the business systems, work system, and human system. These designs are then presented back to the steering team for approval and an implementation plan is developed.

Interactive planning was promoted and written about by Russell Ackoff of the Wharton Business School some years ago. His research showed that when planning was linear, or non-interactive, it produced less change in performance, less results, than when the planning was interactive. An interactive planning model is like a discussion in which

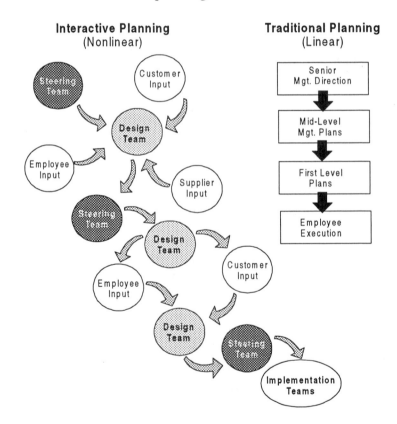

one person says, "I'd like you to do X." And, the second person says, "In other words you want me to do x." And, the first person again says, "Well, not exactly, I would rather it be a bit more like a big X rather than a little x." In a conversation, or in interactive planning, both parties are thinking, contributing and stimulating thoughts in the other. In linear planning the interaction is much more like, "Yes, sir, I'll do it in the morning." And the person may or may not understand what is to be done and makes little contribution to the process of decision-making.

Whole System Architecture, when it is done best, involves a series of interactions, beginning with the steering team presenting the charter to the design team; questions and suggestions by the design team back to the steering team; a second response, etc. It will also involve a series of interactions with the customers, employees, and suppliers. This interactive planning process is nonlinear, it may not follow a straight line, and may appear chaotic at times. It will, however, produce a result that is far more intelligent, with far greater commitment and support by those who must carry out the plan to achieve results. The first step in Whole System Architecture is analyzing the current state of all three subsystems of the organization. Goals and characteristics of the future systems are created after the data are gathered and assessed. What is most critical is that any design or redesign involves integration and alignment of the business, work, and human systems. Any changes made in one system impact changes in other systems. The external environment, customers, competitors, employees, and internal culture are considered when any changes are made to one or all three systems.

Principles of Whole System Architecture

The Founding Fathers, before agreeing on the specific structures of government, first had to be in agreement on the principles of democracy, free expression, and freedom of religion. The structure merely served to fulfill their principles. Whole System Architecture is also principles-based. It is principle-centered redesign. The principles that underlie Whole System Architecture are derived from the best business, management, and psychological theory and practice and are combined in a unique way. These include the principles underlying total quality management, lean production (Toyota Production System), sociotechnical systems, and other practices that have revolutionized the work place to achieve superior quality, productivity, and job satisfaction. Whole System Architecture is a methodology for implementing these systems.

1. Organizations Are Open Systems

Open systems have porous boundaries, are interdependent, and interactive with the environment. The organization is made up of three subsystems, and the alignment of these systems is critical for achieving business results.

Because every corporation is an open system constantly impacted by both internal and external environments, there is an element of chaos, an apparent lack of control. But just as in the free economy, the apparent chaos of this constant interaction conforms to constant principles. The ability to adapt and respond lead to durability of the system.

2. Shared Principles Create Unity

Shared principles cause behavior to be predictable in any social system. Shared principles foster alignment and compatibility of systems, processes, and people and must be applied at all levels and across all functions of the organization. Most significant change results from a change in fundamental principles. The transition from the family farm and craft shop to mass production was based on new principles and priorities. The quality movement changed some of the basic assumptions held by organizations. The belief in the customer as the source of judgment resulted in significant advances. The change from principles of centralized information control to distributed, web-based information distribution is a major shift. Team-based organizations assume principles of shared information, first level decision-making, and frequent process improvement. If you want significant improvement, define and live by your principles.

Cultures change most successfully when the change process is based on the assumption that "we are all in this together," a unity forged by shared principles. If the change process is imposed from the top onto those below without the top demonstrating their participation in the change, disunity is created.

3. Process Will Be Compatible With Result

The process used for designing the organization should be compatible with how the organization will function in the future. From the moment an organization starts a design process, the change process begins. Chaos theory tells us that initial conditions have a large impact on outcomes. Therefore, the process used to manage change, from strategy development to implementation, influences the outcome of the design. If you want an organization that involves people, involve people in the design. If you want an organization that is built on everyone having input and responsibility, use all levels of the organization to design the future state.

4. Provide Minimum Critical Specifications

The design should provide minimal critical specifications to create a flexible organization. The outcome of the first stages of a design process is a blueprint for the organization of the future. This blueprint provides the recommendations for an outline, major components, and a picture of the future organization. An architect must decide where walls go and where wires and plumbing will run through the wall, but does not decide which carpet or wall covering will be used or where the furniture will be placed. When redesigning the organization and its systems the design team will often ask, "Is this a wall or furniture?"

5. Design to Customer Requirements

The customers' needs and business results should be paramount to the design. All work must be designed with the customer in mind. We recommend involving customers in the design of the work processes. In several cases we have had customers dedicate individuals to serve either full or part-time on a design team to provide the most seamless process flow from supplier to customer. You can include them through questionnaires, focus groups, or large-scale conferences. By designing the work processes to meet customers' needs, quality is built into the work. The organization is then formed around the work process to enhance and add value to the work process and the customer. Team structures should be designed with the intent of continuous improvement, process knowledge, and control.

6. Design to Create Shareholder Value

Equally important is designing the future organization to achieve business results. We mentioned earlier the importance of aligning the design process to business strategy and financial. A business organization exists to meet the needs of shareholders as well as customers. To create shareholder value those designing the organization need to understand the business process, the strategy, and financial targets for the future. Many reengineering or socio-technical design efforts were not conducted with a clear focus on creating business results. This lack of connection led to designs not being implemented at all, poorly implemented, or implemented without producing results.

7. Meet Human Needs and Values

Appreciation and understanding of human needs and values should be reflected in the design. Humans have needs for purpose, bonding, recognition, and control of their destiny. Past experience and research have revealed that people will form groups even in environments that do not have formal teams. Teamwork is an outgrowth of the human need to form families, tribes, communities, or clubs. Humans work best in environments that fulfill a need for purpose or meaning. The popularity and success of teams in organizations reflect these underlying needs. When designing the future organization this need for a sense of worthy purpose must be considered.

The need for purpose is never fulfilled by a focus on self, but by focusing on the ability to satisfy others. In business we call those whom we serve "customers." One internal impact of the quality movement was that the focus on customer service helped clarify the sense of mission for which each individual labors each day.

8. There Is No One Right Way

There is no one way to design an organization to achieve its goals. Just as each organization has its own culture and practices, there are many viable alternatives to an organization design. There are many routes to the same goal, and each organization must decide what is best for it. Managers often change structure with no impact on performance, failing to change the more significant work process, competencies, or systems that drive the process. There are an infinite number of possible arrangements of people, teams, information, or work processes. The design team should seek major improvement without the burden to find the one final solution.

9. Design an Adaptive Organization

Change is the only certainty. Within one year the environment, either economic or technology, will impose new forces requiring adaptation. Organizations and people must continually change, improve, and adapt. The redesigned organization must provide for this. The design process by nature is incomplete.

The most critical competitive advantage today is the ability to change rapidly in response to change in the environment. This is why organizations must adopt a philosophy of continuous improvement to survive. This is why a stable, frozen organization will not be able to compete in the future. Only dynamic and adaptive organizations will be able to survive and thrive in a constantly changing world.

10. Designed by the World's Greatest Experts

At Honda the employees who have their "hands on" the work, who are "on-the-spot", are regarded as the "world's greatest experts" in their work. Organizations should be designed by the "world's greatest experts." The majority of organizations have been designed by consultants or senior managers who are often too far removed from the work to understand the requirements of the work process. Change is imposed on those working in the organization and opportunities for valuable input is lost. The Whole System Architecture process is based on the assumption that those who live in the organization and who are intimate with the work are in the best position to design their own process and organization.

11. Design Outside the Village

Design to an ideal or future state beyond your "village." If you ask those who inhabit a New England village to design the ideal house, what is the probability that they will design a Chinese or Japanese style house? Virtually zero. Similarly, if you ask a group in a Japanese or Chinese village to design the ideal house, what is the probability that they will design a house found in a New England village? We all have mental maps that define our village. To design a "world-class" ideal, the members of the design team must escape their village.

The Steering Team: Members, Roles, and Responsibilities

Whole System Architecture is a process that requires deliberate management and leadership. The senior managers of the organization to be redesigned are those who have the power to decide on significant changes in the organization and its systems. These senior managers, and in union environments senior union officials, form the steering team that provides guidance and final decision-making for the change process.

"Who should be on the steering team?" is usually one of the first questions asked. Before we can answer that question, one must answer, "What is the scope of the transformation process?" Is it for a department? A division? A plant? An entire corporation? Once you know the scope and boundaries of the system, you can decide who is on the steering team. It is our recommendation that the senior management team of the organization that will be redesigned should form the steering team. If you are working in a plant, the plant leadership team should all be on the steering team. If you are doing an entire company, the senior executives of the company should be the steering team.

There can be more than one steering team at different levels of the organization. For example, there may be a steering team for the manufacturing division with six plants. There may also be an additional steering team for each of the plants. We facilitated the redesign of an entire major pharmaceutical firm. There was a steering team for the research organization, manufacturing, and sales and marketing. There were other steering teams for human resources, legal, information technology, and other support organizations. On each steering team were executives from customer or supplier organizations. For example, the steering team for the research organization included the senior executive of sales and marketing. The critical point was to create linkage and alignment among the teams and their members. Each of these high-level steering teams then appointed and wrote charters for design teams for their processes.

If there is a union, the union president should be on the steering team. The union should be invited to participate at this level because the design process will inevitably get into contractual issues and working conditions that concern the union. Our experience is that the union can be a valuable ally and an asset if involved early in the process. If they are ignored and surprised by the design they will understandably become an obstacle.

Why are the senior managers and top leaders on the steering team? Why not have lower level employees on the steering team? There are some cases where it may be feasible to include some first-level employees. It is important to understand that the steering team must be that group with the power to make the changes that will be within the scope of the charter. For example, the transformation process will normally consider definition of employee and management positions, the possibility of combining departments and functions, changing compensation, and other significant issues. The steering team must have the power to change these. The members must also be prepared to discuss these issues with absolute frankness and honesty and reach a consensus.

The following are the basic responsibilities of the steering team:

1. Become educated champions: Steering team members need education and knowledge to be able to lead and champion the change effort. This includes training about Whole System Architecture, team management, and strategy. They must be the champions of the change, not just the supporters.

2. Develop and communicate the business system and strategy: This responsibility is an ongoing one. The business system drives the change effort and the competitive advantage of the organization.

3. Write and communicate the Whole System Architecture charter: The charter provides the foundation for the transformation process. The steering team must write it, own it, and communicate it.

4. Meet as a team, practice team skills, and improve own work: All these tasks cannot be accomplished unless the steering team learns to function as a high-performance team. This happens with training, practice, and coaching.

5. Meet regularly with design team(s): We usually advise the steering team to meet with the design team informally on a regular basis for updates and questions and for more formal presentations at major milestones. There is a tendency for design teams to get ahead of steering teams in knowledge, thinking, and creativity if these teams do not stay in communication with each other.

6. Serve as boundary managers for the transformation process with the rest of the organization: The steering team must help the design team and the transformation process become integrated with the rest of the organization. The organization can reject the design team and the process. If the organization does not understand and support the change, it can reject the design team and the process. The steering team is responsible for managing boundaries with other parts of the organization to ensure acceptance, not rejection, of the process and outcomes.

7. Accept, reject, or modify recommendations from design team(s): The steering team makes the final decisions about what recommendations will be implemented. It is its responsibility to make timely decisions and communicate them to keep the change process moving properly. Because the steering team must be responsible for implementation, the whole team needs to be involved in approving the final plan for the future organization.

8. Provide support, resources, and guidance throughout the WSA process: Throughout the WSA process, there will be competition for time and resources. It will seem hard to balance the resource needs for the present operation and the time required to design for the future. The steering team must help provide the support, people, money, and time for both to happen. Their time, expertise, and attention will be needed from the time the strategy is developed through the final stages of implementation.

9. Communicate regularly with the organization: Leading is an active role. It requires face-to-face time with people in small groups or large conferences. All members of the steering team need to be visibly involved to demonstrate unity of effort and focus.

10. Provide consequences for actions: People do what they are reinforced for doing. If they are told to do something, do not do it, and nothing happens to them, they will believe they do not have to do it. Therefore, there need to be positive, rewarding consequences for people who are supporting the change effort. And, there need to be negative consequences and feedback to those who fight the change or do not complete assignments. If the steering team ignores undesirable behavior (steering team members not attending meetings or managers bad-mouthing the change process), there will be an increase of counterproductive behaviors.

Design Team: Members, Roles, and Responsibilities

The detailed work of WSA is best done by a dedicated design team. They might meet every week for two or three days, every other week for four days, or every day each week. The amount of time they spend on the task depends on the scope of work and how quickly the design must be completed. Even if they are not in meetings, they may collect data, meet with other employees, or do benchmarking trips. A design team functions best when they have a room in which to work, store materials, and leave things hanging on the wall. The productivity and efficiency of the design team is enhanced by administrative support.

A design team is typically eight to fourteen people. At least half are typically first-level employees who are "hands-on" and are expert in the work. It is useful to consider having a steering team member on the design team. This person is not the leader but a participant on the team. This individual must be exceptionally good at listening, not taking charge, and encouraging others to contribute. This individual can serve as a liaison to and from the steering team. Supervisors, subject matter experts, and other resources can be on the team. Look for a cross-section of the organization to be design team members. If there is a union, you want members of the union on the team.

The following are the responsibilities of the design team members:

1. Be an active, responsible member of the team: To be an effective member of the team, one must be at meetings, complete action assignments, and manage his or her regular work. The steering team is responsible for making resources available, and the design team members are responsible for balancing their overall time.

2. Do benchmarking: Team members have to go on trips, talk to other companies, or do research to learn best-practices. They must be able to learn from these experiences and share them with the other team members.

3. Communicate with other employees: Through informal and formal means, design team members must communicate with others in the organization. The design team members gather information, ask questions, and listen to what other people in the organization think about the current and future organization.

4. Define current state work and human systems: It is hard work to define the current operation, map processes, and understand current cycle times and other measurements. The members do this as a team, as subgroups, and as individuals.

5. Analyze variances and data: The team analyzes and critiques the current ways things are done to find opportunities for improvement and breakthroughs. They use a variety of tools and methods to accomplish this.

6. Define the future or ideal state for work and human systems: The design team creates a design for the future organization. They share these ideas with the others in the company and with the steering team and receive feedback.

7. Make presentations: The design team makes informal presentations to people about the transformation process. They also make formal presentations to the steering team at certain intervals throughout the process (e.g., at the end of the work process design).

8. Be a change champion: The design team members serve as champions for the change. They help persuade and sell others on their design and help people understand the benefits of the new organization.

Chapter Two
Defining the Business System & Scorecard

The process of Whole System Architecture has been developed and tested over several decades. The following steps provide a general roadmap for the work of the design team. There is a tendency for some to turn their brains off and follow a defined process without questioning the order of steps, timing, or depth of analysis. Every organization is different. They have different personalities, operate in unique environments, and have unique histories. While we encourage following this process, we do so with the small caveat that you must still use your good judgment! Questioning the steps and plan for redesigning the organization will create understanding and improvement. After all, this entire process is the result of our own learning from experience, learning from our clients.

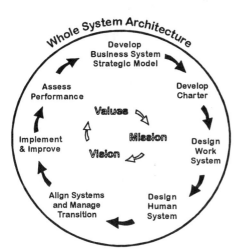

The process of change begins with and assessment of current performance and the understanding and commitment of the leadership team. This leadership team may develop the business strategy or call upon a strategy design team to study the environment, current capabilities, assess challenges and opportunities and develop a strategic business model. Based on approval of this strategy, the leadership team will then write an organization design charter. This charter will define the future capabilities required to implement the strategy. They will then appoint a design team to do the detailed analysis and design of the future work and human systems. It is not unusual for this work to take six or eight months.

Their work will go more quickly if they have skilled and experienced facilitation that can guide them through this process without wasting time. Here are the seven key steps in the process:

1. Develop a business system strategic model: The business system is the flow of money, input and output, and an under-

standing of what causes inputs and outputs to increase and decrease, and a plan for how to improve business performance over the next several years. This model and plan connect the process of improvement in the work system and the human system to financial performance. This development of strategy and business model can be done by the steering team itself or by an appointed strategy design team that will report its results to the steering team for decision.

2. The steering team develops the charter for aligning the organization to the strategy.

3. The work system, which is the work processes measured by quality, cycle time, costs and productivity, is analyzed and redesigned (or reengineered) by the design team.

4. The human system is everything concerning people. It is the hiring, training, motivating, managing, organizing and learning of people. The human systems should be designed to support the strategy and the work system.

5. At each stage of the process the design team will share its results with the steering team. After all three systems have been redesigned and approved, an implementation plan will be developed.

6. Implementation may be immediate or extend over several years depending on the complexity and costs of implementation. The implementation process will be a learning experience and that learning should be processed in the spirit of "continuous improvement."

7. Performance should be assessed both before and after the whole system redesign process. Measures of financial performance, process performance and human factors should all be evaluated to assess the impact of the changes.

The following is more detailed description of the process of redesigning the three major subsystems of the organization – the business system, the work system, and the human system.

Business System Strategy & Scorecard

The purpose of strategy is to define how the organization will create value - value to customers and shareholders, and to define the key internal changes that must occur to create this value.

Operational Effectiveness Versus Strategic Value:

Most organizations have been improving. They have improved their effectiveness in listening and responding to their customers, they have reduced unnecessary costs, have improved cycle times from design to delivery, and generally have become more effective. This, however, does not assure their success and survival. Their success and survival will be based, not only on effectiveness, but on their ability to create superior value. Creating superior value requires doing the right things to add value in the customer's perception, doing things that create uniqueness and that are not so easily imitated. This ability to create superior value for the customer is quickly recognized in the market place and therefore creates shareholder value. This is the strategic advantage.

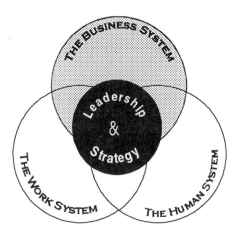

Many companies want to jump into redesigning processes, organizations, and systems without any strategic understanding of how they will create value. They want to make these improvements because they know that the organization and its processes can and need to be improved. They may be responding to customer complaints or the recognition that their competitors are faster or lower cost. These improvements may well be desirable. They are, however, operational improvements not strategic improvements. They are "keeping-up-with-the-Joneses" improvements. They are reactive and fail to add any unique source of value that will impact long-term business performance.

Improved effectiveness can create a sufficient leap in improvement so that it does enhance value. When McDonald's redefined the small restaurant business, they applied Henry Ford's principles of simplicity and low cost production to hamburgers, this was such a significant leap in effectiveness that it created new value for customers and shareholders. When Honda applied the principles of continuous improvement in a manner that created an entirely unique culture in its manufacturing facilities, they not only improved effectiveness, they created value by creating a difficult-to-copy competitive advantage. On the other hand, many quality improvement efforts, including most of those in the U.S. auto industry, improved effectiveness but created no unique competitive strength. Whole System Architecture begins with a vision of how the organization can create a significant improvement in value, a strategic competitive advantage. Then the work processes and organizational systems are designed to enable the creation of this new value.

Who Owns Strategy?

It is traditionally assumed that strategy belongs to the most senior executives. It is their job to decide where their company is going, to create a strategic vision. Others are responsible for implementing and executing the strategy. While this view will always be true in some measure, there is a new reality. Professional employees with competitive skills, transportable from company to company, will not be content to simply trust in senior management's strategic wisdom. They know better. They know that the most senior managers are not the sole owners of great thoughts, dreams, imagination, and creativity. In fact, the best visions of what is possible in the future often come from those who are directly working on new technologies or working directly with customers. One of the reasons many strategies are never implemented is because they were created by the senior managers without involvement of those close to the work and therefore did not reflect the realities on the ground. Today the best strategic planning process is a dynamic dialogue that involves managers and employees at various levels as they create a common vision of the future organization.

A Process View of Strategy

Strategy is not a piece of paper stating a plan. It is not a single goal. It is not a set of goals. Strategy is a way of thinking about the organization and its future. Strategy is alive, organic, and in motion. Strategy is not static, but dynamic. Our culture tends to focus on things, objects, rather than appreciation of a living process. We tend to focus on the instrument rather than the music. Managers want to have the "thing" called a strategic plan so they can feel a sense of accomplishment and completion, rather than be continually engaged in the "process" of living strategy. Having a strategic plan can quickly result in the return to normal habits because the plan is "done." "Done" often means quickly forgotten. Engagement in the process of strategy is never "done." It is a daily pursuit, a daily thought process, and a daily concern. Strategic leaders think differently than operating managers. Strategic leaders are constantly engaged in thinking about the strategy of the organization - constantly thinking about how the organization will create future value.

A process model describes the interdependent relationships between different activities within a system. You will recall our systems model of the Whole System Architecture. To the left is a process model for strategy development. Processes may be either linear or nonlinear. A linear process is consistently ordered, with "A" always followed by "B," which is then followed by "C," etc. In a nonlinear process you may still have steps "A," "B," and "C." However, sometimes it may make most sense for "B" to come first, then followed by "C," and finally "A." This may seem chaotic, but in the real world in which human beings and their organizations develop, processes are often nonlinear. For example, an organization may discover in the middle of the implementation of a strategy that a competitor has developed a new technical capability that gives them a unique advantage. Should the organization wait until the beginning of the strategy process cycle to consider a response to this threat? Of course not. It is easy to imagine dozens of other examples of external or internal events, the discovery of new technologies, the merger of competitors, the loss of a significant client, etc., that may necessitate reconsideration of the strategy.

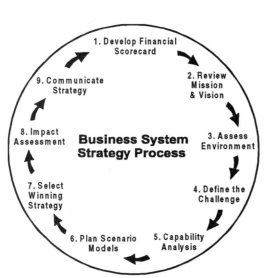

In this Leader's Guide we will not go through the details of every step of this process. You can refer to the Change Management workbook for this. We will highlight some of the key understandings that are most important for the leaders.

1. Develop a Financial Scorecard

You can't play the game without a scorecard! The game of business is like any other game. Behavior, motivation, and fun are derived from watching the scorecard and doing your best to win. The scorecard must be linked to meet the needs of both customers and shareholders.

One of the favorite words of modern management language is "stakeholder," a reference to all of those who have an interest in the well being and behavior of the corporation. Customers, environmental groups, government, employee groups, suppliers, and others are stakeholders who have an interest in the performance of the organization. However, there are two, and only two, one thousand pound gorillas in the community of stakeholders. There is serious danger among managers, consultants and others involved in the change process to be distracted by other stakeholders and failing to listen for the heavy footsteps of a gorilla. The two gorillas are the customers and owners. When these two gorillas feel that they are not being listened to they become anxious. Failing to keep an eye on an anxious gorilla has altered more than one career plan. The redesign of the organizations systems and structure to constantly be measured against the standard of creating value for customers and shareholders. Satisfaction of employees, the community, and other stakeholders should also be considered, but survival depends on revenue and capital, customers and shareholders.

The lifeblood of every corporation is capital and revenue. Capital comes from shareholders, revenue from customers. The strategy of every corporation must be built on an understanding of how the requirements of these two groups can be met or exceeded.

What do the owners really want? If you can answer this question, you are well on your way to establishing a basic criterion of strategy. The most significant measure of how well a chief executive is performing these days is his or her contribution to shareholder value. What is the shareholder's investment worth today versus a year earlier? The value of the investment is determined primarily by three measures: the rate of revenue growth, the rate of return, and the security or stability of the investment. Every strategy meets some combination of these needs.

In order to help communicate the financial targets that will guide the strategic plan, it may be helpful to illustrate the financial position and movement of the organization. The illustrated matrix reflects the two key variables that drive shareholder value: revenue growth and rate of return. Stock price reflects current and anticipated future movement of these two variables. How well your company's stock does is a reflection of the perception that your "investor's dot" is moving northeast at a rate superior to that of your competition. Plot the dot for your revenue growth and rate of return on assets for at least three years. In which direction is the dot moving?

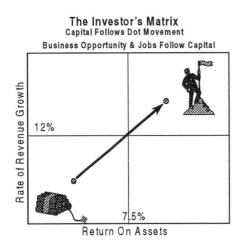

The Investor's Matrix
Capital Follows Dot Movement
Business Opportunity & Jobs Follow Capital

If possible, plot the dot movement of your most significant competitors? Whose dot movement is most likely to make the gorilla smile? Where does your investor's dot need to move over the next five years in order to continue to attract capital?

Once you understand where your company falls in terms of its relative financial performance then you can ask the question - "what do we have to do to move the dot northeast?" The answer to this simple question is a key element of a strategic business model.

Up to this point we have simply been asking, "What kind of financial performance do we need to achieve? What rate of revenue growth and rate of return are required by the shareholders?" The answer to these questions provides a general basis for a financial strategy; however, it does not provide sufficient detail to explain exactly how we will achieve those results. Exactly what products will produce increased revenue? What expenses can be reduced to enhance return to the shareholders? How can we utilize our assets more efficiently?

A Language of Financial Strategy

1. Strategic Business Model: A description of how the business will create shareholder value. This description includes identification of markets, products or services, and a financial analysis demonstrating how enhanced revenue growth and/or return on assets will be achieved. The business model may also include the definition of specific revenue, expense and asset utilization targets, and value drivers.

2. Business Plan or Scorecard: A business plan is typically developed annually by managers as a statement of business goals, priorities, and actions for the coming year to achieve financial, marketing, and operational performance. The business plan should be derived from the business model and include those targets for revenue enhancement, expenses and asset utilization that will enhance shareholder value. This serves as a scorecard for management and for the design team in their efforts to redesign the system to enhance value to both customers and shareholders.

3. Financial Targets: A financial target is a specific revenue, expense, or asset level goal based on a specific line item of the financial statement, which you believe will result in significantly improved value to the shareholder. To move your dot northeast you need to have knowledge of the contributing factors. These appear on the Profit and Loss statement that reports revenues and expenses as well as the balance statement that reports assets held. From these statements you can identify key financial targets that can be improved. Selecting key financial measures and setting targets for the following three years is recommended.

4. Value Drivers: Value drivers are those critical operations of performance, which can be measured, that will positively impact a specific financial target. In order to achieve the financial targets, some operations must be improved. The behavior of employees and managers drives financial performance and adds value.

Example: In a fast food restaurant a financial target may be an increase in revenue from dessert sales. The value driver that will impact this financial performance is the behavior of employees offering the dessert to each customer.

Essentially, three types of performance "move the dot." The first is revenue. Business unit revenue appears as the first major set of numbers on the P&L statement. The second set of numbers is the expense items. Obviously, if revenue is greater than expenses, there is a profit. If not, there is a loss. The balance sheet reports the assets held by the company. These are the numbers studied by every serious investor who is attempting to value the business.

The steering team and/or design team will now take the P&L statement and identify key performance targets for revenue, expenses and asset utilization. They will then, for each target, identify value drivers, those specific performances that will cause the target to be achieved. The value drivers point to the work processes that must be improved in order to achieve the targets of the strategy.

The strategy may be to be among the top three in volume sales in a market. In order to close the gap from current sales to that required to be one of the three market leaders will require specific improvements in performance. For example, a value driver for increasing sales may be to increase sales calls made on prospects, or to improve quality measures by a specific amount. These performances will now become a focus of the design team as they translate business strategy into work process improvement and human systems improvement.

2. Review Mission & Vision

By now every company and organization in the world must have developed a mission and vision statement. Mission is the purpose for which the organization exists. Mission statements will usually reflect the organization's purpose as meeting the needs of stockholders, communities, and employees. Vision is a snapshot of the future, or strategic intent. It is self-evident that the strategy of the organization and the organizational structure and systems should be aligned with the mission and vision.

In too many organizations, there is little relationship between the stated missions and vision and how the organization actually behaves. The strategy process should seek to create alignment between the stated mission and vision and actual behavior within the organization. There is a logical flow from a general understanding of mission or purpose and a vision of what it will be like in the future, to a more specific plan and strategy to achieve the vision. At this point it only makes sense to review these two statements, develop them if they do not exist, and then proceed to create the strategy using these statements as building blocks.

The mission statement should...

- Address "why" you exist.
- Address what business you are in.
- Cover core purpose.
- Cover aspirations with respect to stakeholders.
- Reflect values and principles.

The mission statement may include...

- What business are we in?
- What competencies and capabilities will we provide?
- What is our purpose?
- How do we provide value?
- What makes us unique?

Vision is a look forward. You use your eyes in the front of your head therefore, vision is in front of you. What will your organization look like, feel like, or be viewed as by outsiders, in five to ten years? If you were at a social gathering five years from now and were engaged in a discussion about your company, how would you describe its business and culture? Vision Statements Are...

- From the heart.
- Authentic and personal.
- Able to create guiding principles.
- Able to create uniqueness.
- More than just words.
- Able to be visualized by employees, customers and share-holders.

3. Assess the Environment

Good business managers, no matter what type of business, have a sure-shot-super-detective radar screen scanning the environment. A pilot of a ship does not set a course across the ocean and then put the ship on automatic pilot. Someone is "on-watch," constantly scanning the horizon and watching the radar screen for storms, other ships, and obstacles. Similarly, in business, someone must be "on-watch" constantly scanning the external environment for signals that require a new course.

The external environment is itself a system. It includes the pull of market forces and social, political, and economic trends. It includes the chaos caused by new technologies and the often unpredictable behavior of competitors. These forces represent a complex dynamic system. Each of these forces is impacting the other. The trend toward deregulation is as much a matter of social sentiments as it is the writing of regulations. The trend toward working at home is linked to the women's movement, the availability of talent in professional areas, and development of computer technology that enables networked locations. These are interactive components of the external system.

4. Defining the Challenge

One way of understanding strategy is to see it as a challenge-and-response mechanism; the response producing a wave pattern of success or failure, each wave in its turn presenting a new challenge. Creatively responding to challenge is the essence of strategy. The challenge may be presented by the external environment. It may be a new technology, a shift in market preference, a decline in a market, or behavior of competitors. The challenge can come from within. The challenge may be the self-recognition that one's technology is aging or the creativity on the part of employees to recognize a better way to meet customer needs. Companies often decline, not because of brilliant moves by a competitor, but because of their own loss of motivation and creativity. Bureaucratic companies lose the ability to respond, they lose the force of will, the ability of self-determination. Bureaucracies essentially commit suicide rather than suffer defeat at the hands of external barbarians.

Companies also fail because they recognize a challenge but fail to create the internal alignment, harmony within, which permits an effective response. A company such as Sears, may have originally been a creative company and responded to the challenge of a dispersed marketplace. However, Sears grew accustomed to its market position. Suddenly, an aggressive newcomer, Wal-Mart, creates new responses to the challenge of the market. These responses were clearly visible, but the culture of Sears, seen from the height of the Sears Tower, was not able to exert it will and respond successfully. Sears lacked alignment of vision, strategy and structure. The mind and the body were not pointed in the same direction. Intellectually, Sears knew it had to change its ways, but the systems and structure of the company made this almost impossible. The U.S. auto companies suffered similar experiences, as did IBM. The recognition of challenge and the idea of a successful response to challenge is not adequate. The internal mechanism, the culture, must be realigned to the realities of the new battle.

To this point in your search for strategy, you have gathered information on the environment – the financial and market requirements and the forces of political, social, technological, and economic changes that may influence your future. It is now time to look at that information and consider its significance. Which of the facts that you have uncovered represents the greatest challenge to the organization? Which facts represent threats to your market position? Which represent challenging opportunities? Which, if not met, will result in the loss of economic viability?

You now must make judgments. What represent the greatest challenge. A challenge may be either a threat, opportunity or both. A challenge requires a significant response, a change in the way you approach your market.

5. Assess Your Capabilities

Good strategy applies the principles of leverage. If you are developing a game plan for a football team and you know that you have the world's best offensive line, your game plan will leverage these assets against your opponent. If you know that your quarterback has a weak arm and your receivers are mediocre, it would be foolish to develop a game plan that relied heavily on a passing offense.

Every business has assets. Its assets may include plant and equipment, property, cash in the bank, or a strong credit rating. Often the most important assets are the human competencies of the organization. There are competencies in most organizations that may be called "core competencies" or "core capabilities." These are the competencies essential to the core processes. Core capabilities contribute most to economic value.

If you are Merck or Pharmacia & Upjohn, your core competence is the research and development of new drugs. If you are Disney, you have core competencies in creative entertainment and customer service. It is only logical that those processes that contribute most to creating economic value are also those in which you have developed a high degree of competence.

Based on your understanding of the challenges facing the organization that you have already identified, you will want to consider whether both these processes and competencies are those necessary in the future. It is normal in business that competencies that once produced the most significant market impact no longer have the same impact. IBM's sales force used to be the world's most respected. In the world of mainframe computers and proprietary software platforms, that sales force represented both a core process and a core competence. In the world of Intel, Microsoft, and Dell Computers, that same sales force no longer has the same value.

The forces in the environment impact the necessity of capabilities. As the economic, political, technical, and social forces shift, so too does the need for capabilities. It is precisely for this reason that strategy is a dynamic rather than static process. Successful companies are constantly shifting, developing, and abandoning capabilities as they recognize shifts in their environments.

Capability Planning Process		
Current Capabilities ➡	**Strategic Scenarios** ➡	**Future Capability Requirements**
Current Technical Capabilities	Analysis of financial and market requirements, social, political, economic and technology trends, competitor benchmarking and assessment of organization capabilities leading to the selection of future strategic scenarios.	Future Technical Capabilities
Current Human Capabilities		Future Human Capabilities

Technical Capabilities

Technical capabilities include work processes, equipment, and physical assets. The technical systems are the systems that define how we get the work done. Producing a profit-and-loss statement is an output of a work process in the accounting department. If that work is completed with only the assistance of a mechanical adding machine, it may be capable of delivering a report thirty days after the end of the month. If a computer and accounting software are purchased, the system may now be capable of delivering the report by the tenth day of the month. This is improved technical capability.

Capabilities must correspond to the value desired by the marketplace. The capability to deliver a package within hours is desired by business shippers. The capability to provide clear and immediate telephone access is desired by telephone customers. The ability to transmit data communications is increasingly a capability requirement for long distance carriers.

Human Capabilities

Capabilities include many things. For a fast food chain it may include properties that will allow it to reach its customers. It will include equipment and technology. However the single most critical capability that will distinguish competitors is human competence. For every organization there are core competencies which are critical to its strategic competitive success.

Virtually every company can borrow money or buy equipment. Human talent, competence, and commitment are the most difficult capabilities to acquire and, therefore, the greatest competitive advantage. Products and services result from the mind of creative and committed people. The competencies that are most critical to the business strategy are called the "core competencies." *Core competencies are those that are essential to the creation of strategic value.*

Market leaders tend to be those organizations with the best-developed core competencies and high-rate learning organizations. This should be a key goal of the development of organizational architecture.

High-rate learning must occur at every level and in every function of the organization. Most important to competitive strategy is the learning and nurturing of the core competencies around which the organization's products and markets revolve. Honda pursues a strategy of nurturing and developing engine technology. They value, invest in, and promote the people who pursue and advance that technology. Canon has developed new products as a result of its superior competence in optics. For years Procter & Gamble was the world's leading expert in consumer marketing.

C.K. Prahalad and Gary Hamel wrote recently in the *Harvard Business Review, "In the long run, competitiveness derives from an ability to build at lower cost and more speedily than competitors the core competencies that spawn unanticipated products. The real sources of advantage are to be found in management's ability to consolidate corporate wide technologies and production skills into competencies that empower individual businesses to adapt quickly to changing opportunities.... Both the theory and practice of Western management have created a drag on our forward motion. It is the principles of management that are in need of reform."*

Peter Drucker said that business has only two functions: innovation and marketing. Innovation comes first. Strategy requires knowing where innovation is likely to come from and preparing the soil and planting the seeds. The rich soil of innovation is found in the core competencies of the organization. It is a strategic imperative of management today to develop the organization's core competencies.

6. Scenario Planning

Royal Dutch Shell gained some fame for their strategic scenario planning process. They are credited with developing scenarios that predicted the fall of communism and the opening of the Soviet Union when the CIA, with supposedly superior intelligence, told them they were crazy. Shell and other petroleum companies make multi-billion dollar investments that often have a ten to twenty year pay back period and are precariously built on assumptions about the future price of a barrel of oil. The price of oil is affected by political, economic, technical, and social trends. It was, therefore, particularly important to Shell to anticipate these changes. Scenario planning has continued as a regular component of strategic planning, and Shell involves a large number of managers at many levels of the company.

The impact of this scenario planning is not simply the development of better strategy but the education and development of thinking skills among Shell's managers. Shell engages its managers in disciplined thinking about the future. The process of developing business system strategy is just such a disciplined process.

Once your team has considered the financial and market requirements, the environmental influences, and defined the key challenges facing the organization, it is ready to define potential responses to those challenges. These responses, the implications for the organization, and the resulting interaction with the environment are the scenarios that can be the basis for a strategy.

7. Select a Winning Strategy

Based on the assessment of challenges, the definition of scenarios representing potential responses, and the financial analysis, the management team now should be prepared to select what they believe will be the winning strategy or strategies. It is absolutely essential at this stage for the leader to challenge the group to genuinely commit to the pursuit of these strategies with significant energy. Very often, management groups go through strategic planning exercises, identify what they believe to be winning strategies, and then fail to pursue them. At some point, all of the analysis, surveys, matrices, and data gathering will not replace the need for strong leadership and decision-making.

8. Impact Assessment

As the initial scenarios are developed, the top three or four alternatives will emerge. Each of the strategic scenarios will represent investment and cost-benefit decisions. A small team should be put together to become advocates for each potential scenario. For the three or four scenarios, a team of champions should be identified. It is wise to ask for volunteers who are enthusiastic about pursuing a strategic scenario, and let them develop a financial plan with investments at rates of return projected.

9. Communicate the Strategy

Remember that there is little inherent value in a strategy. Value is in its deployment, its implementation. The definition and design of organization capabilities, both the technical capabilities and human capabilities, are essential to the deployment of the strategy. The following chapters of this book define a process for deploying strategy.

Pursuing strategy is not only committing to investments, designing work processes, and human systems. It also requires marketing. The concept of internal marketing is rarely understood in organizations. The idea of communicating image, emotions, and dream, is well understood when marketing a product to a consumer in order to motivate buying behavior. Internally, any new strategy requires similar marketing.

Years ago we worked with an organization in Florida that was a division of Dun & Bradstreet. The company was started by a colorful entrepreneur named Jack Murray. Jack was a great motivator and highly successful at building companies. He had a goal of reaching one billion dollars in revenue by the end of a year. This is one case in which every single employee was highly aware, every day, of the goal and the progress made toward the goal. There was one lobby and entrance to the building in which most of the employees worked. When you walked into the front entrance you were confronted with a huge mountain, the "One Billion Dollar Mountain" right there in the lobby! Jack had this constructed with a little mountain climber ascending the side of the mountain. When employees turned on their computer terminals the first thing they saw was...guess what? The "One Billion Dollar Mountain" with the mountain climber making progress and the current revenue level indicated alongside the climber. There were regular celebrations of benchmark levels toward the peak of the mountain. Anyone unaware of the single over-riding goal of the company had to be sleepwalking.

Chapter Three

Designing the Work System

Reengineering, the Toyota Production System, and the quality management movement have stimulated a great deal of attention to improving work processes. Much of this is good, yet efforts to improve work processes have frequently been unsuccessful. There are three reasons for this. First, the work process is usually analyzed and changed separately from the business system or the human system. Since the work process is dependent on both of these systems the change efforts fail. Second, those doing reengineering have often assumed that you can divide the work processes, line them up in a straight line, and understand how the work gets done. The problem is that these processes are often so interdependent that they can not be changed independently. Third, all processes are not linear. For example, Frederick Taylor assumed you could observe workers doing their jobs, measure each discrete step with a stop watch, and study how step A was followed by B, etc. More and more of the value-adding work in organizations is knowledge work. It is nonlinear and defies the logic of Tayloristic analysis.

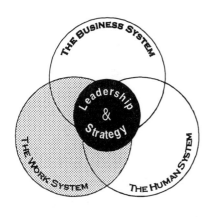

Whole System Architecture provides a new paradigm for designing work processes that corrects for the three previously listed problems. It provides a holistic method for analyzing and redesigning work processes that takes into consideration the interdependency of processes and systems. It also provides ways to analyze and design nonlinear and knowledge work. A brief review of what happened to work will help lead to an understanding of how we must analyze work differently today.

Principles of Work System Design

Today's work system is the result of an accumulation of habits and ideas over the past several decades. Efforts to improve quality and productivity by only telling people to work more carefully and to care about their customers will not produce significant long-term advantages. The organization and its work must be designed based on the principles discussed in this manual. Without a different set of principles, the future organization cannot be more competitive or improve. The following are the principles underlying work system design. As the design team analyzes and designs the future work processes, these principles should be kept in mind.

1. Design to Customers, Strategy, and Targets: Begin the design work with a clear understanding of customer requirements from the customer's point of view. Be sure that the process will achieve a goal linked to the organization's strategy. And be sure that the redesign will help to achieve financial targets linked to the business or department's P&L statement. By starting with a charter that spells out what the strategy, business targets, and customer requirements are, you ensure that the design does this.

2. Eliminate Waste: This is the single most powerful idea behind lean production. Toyota worked for thirty years on the elimination of waste. Most companies have just begun. Study waste in time, materials, space, and activities. Analyze the current processes for waste, and create new or redesigned processes that avoid waste of all kinds. Waste occurs in materials, time, money, and effort or energy lost. Poorly designed systems cause waste. Understanding just-in-time philosophies and incorporating them into redesign plans can help design teams reduce waste of all kinds.

Non-value-adding activity is waste. Eliminate non-value-adding activity. Quality is doing the right things right the first time and every time. Most employees and managers know of things that they could be doing to add value for their customers, but they do not have the time. On the other hand, they spend much of their time doing things that do not add value. The future organization has deployed its assets, particularly its human assets, in a manner that optimizes value-adding activity.

3. Create Continuous Flow: Work that is standing is waste! Work that is in flow is adding value. Processes that have been designed so employees are doing whole work, (building chairs, rather than legs) reduces waste by creating a continuous flow. Walls can be physical or organizational. Walls hinder continuous flow. Walls can be closed doors, material delays, or unnecessary levels of approval and separation of work. Delays increase costs and the opportunity for mistakes and problems which may go undetected. Look for opportunities to connect operations. Design for continuous movement of work.

Organizations that consistently produce high quality are fast. Cycle times of workflow and decision-making have been minimized by eliminating interruptions and non-value-adding work. Speed, quality, and low cost go together.

4. Minimize In-Process Work: Large piles are bad! Small piles are good! Eliminate pallets, bins, and piles on the floor or on desks. Find ways to reduce in-process work. Also look for ways to reduce inventory in general. Just-in-time processes and partnerships with vendors and suppliers provide opportunities for continuous flow and minimizing in-process work. A short walk through a world class manufacturing facility quickly reveals the absence of warehouses and large stocks in in-process inventory. That which is in motion is adding value, eliminate that which is standing.

5. Provide First Level Control: When employees feel control of their work they feel ownership of that work. When they feel ownership they seek improvements. Make sure the correct tools, equipment, technology, and technical training are designed into the work system for people to be able to do exert control and responsibility. Mistake proof (automate and eliminate human error) processes as much as possible.

Many efforts are made to motivate employees. They are offered awards, praise, and promotions and are constantly told why they should be motivated. Most employees are motivated if they feel they have control of their work, if they can improve their work. They become frustrated by their lack of control and lose motivation.

6. Eliminate or Control Causes of Variances: Variances are problems, deviations from standard or best practice. Variances are the cause quality problems, rework, delays, frustration, and waste. Study and eliminate the causes of variances. Most quality problems are system problems. They may occur at the level of the individual employee or machine, but they are the result of that person or machine working within a system that has not been designed to eliminate the causes of quality variances. Many variances cannot be eliminated within the operation of a system and must be controlled at their source. If you cannot eliminate a variance and its cause, design the work so someone doing the job can catch and fix the variance immediately.

7. Design with Information in Mind: Design the work system so those doing the work will have complete access to all information needed. Find opportunities to change and improve information technology and information flows. Look for ways to capture information automatically and make it readily available for people who need it to do their jobs. Specify information requirements for processes and technology systems.

Information increases learning. Learning is the result of a system that is designed to provide knowledge, particularly data-based feedback on recent performance and on the reaction by the customer to the output of the system. The organization's design should result in the creation of a "learning organization," one in which learning or continuous improvement is valued and supported by the system.

8. Design the Work System to Facilitate Horizontal Processes as Much as Possible: Try to organize work flows to facilitate whole work. Design around the future or ideal state process. Do not design to existing functions and departments; this limits your thinking

The design team first analyzes the current state of the work processes and systems and then addresses the social systems. Why do they start with the work processes? They start with work processes because this is the reason the organization exists! The organization does not exist to have teams, to conduct performance appraisals, train employees, or pay compensation. It exists to do work for customers.

The Seven Steps of Work System Design

1. Scan the Environment
2. Identify Key Processes, Customers, Suppliers, and Requirements
3. Define the Current State Processes and Work System
4. Analyze the Processes for
   - Speed
   - Quality
   - Cost
   - Principles and Charter
5. Define the Ideal Processes and Work System
6. Analyze Cost/Benefit
7. Get Feedback on New Process Design and Work System

Step 1: Scan the Environment

The design team requires a clear quantitative and qualitative picture, a scan, of the organization's performance and environment.

Part of this scanning was done during the development of the business system and strategy. It continues during the analysis of the work system.

The environmental scan conducted by the design team at this stage covers more detailed and immediate information needed by the design team to do their work. For example, the strategy may be to have a more responsive, fast cycle manufacturing process that can produce batches of one. The design team will need to scan the environment to determine what technologies, skills, data, or information are associated with the current operation and organization. The design team needs current data about how the operation is functioning, information about cycle times, customer satisfaction, and employee attitudes. They need to know what the performance gaps are between the current state and objectives for the future.

The idea of scanning the environment is based on an "open-systems" theory of the organization. This theory assumes that the organization is organic or constantly changing, responding to influences. There is no one right end state; there is an ongoing evolutionary process. To design the optimum future organization, you must understand the current organization. To be able to show improvement or evidence of change you must be able to compare current and future measurement.

There are several possible ways of gathering information on the current environment. A method that has become popular in recent years is the search conference methodology first developed by Eric Trist and Fred Emery and later popularized in this country by Marvin Weisbord (1992, *Discovering Common Ground*. San Francisco: Berrett-Koehler). The primary purpose of this method is to involve as many members of the organization as possible in the development of the new organization design. It may include other stakeholders such as customers and suppliers. This provides not only broad input but also increases buy-in to the end product.

By involving many stakeholders in the search conference, the work of the design team is expedited and pressure on them to represent all the employees is diminished. A great deal of time can be saved by using the conference method. For example, conference participants (about eighty) in a manufacturing plant produced six variations of an ideal state organization structure in two and a half hours. These were just ideas that required greater investigation, but the design team was then able to take this input and define the structure much more quickly than if they had worked alone. Because this structure was the result of common "thinking" developed with a large number of employee members, it had wide acceptance when time came for implementation.

Step 2: Identify Core Processes, Customers, Suppliers, and Requirements

Every organization has hundreds of processes. The critical processes are those that have the greatest impact on the customer. It is these that should be the primary focus of the design team.

On the macro level, the steering committee will have brainstormed the primary or core processes for the entire organization. The core processes answers the question, *"Why does this organization exist? What processes fulfill that purpose?"* Manufacturing the product for the customer is probably a core process. Training employees to work in that process is an ***enabling process***.

The concept of core and enabling processes is important when seeking to design the organizational system. The redesign should begin with a focus on the core processes. Why? Because the core process is that process that results in the output of the system for which customers pay money. The core process is the process that transforms input to output. This is a simple definition, but there is elegant truth in the simplicity. Customers do not write checks because you train your employees well, provide good recognition, have wonderful teams, or the latest and greatest information systems. They pay you money because your product is well designed, engineered, manufactured, and sold. This is the core process.

Core and Enabling Processes

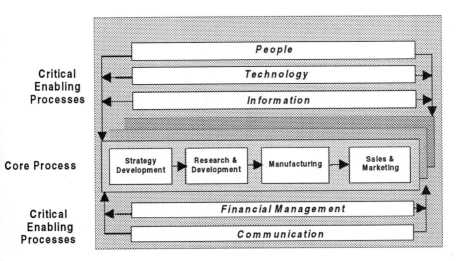

Critical Enabling Processes

Core Process

Critical Enabling Processes

The human resource processes, financial management, information management, and other processes that support the core process may be called enabling processes. They enable the core. This enabling or support role does not imply that they are not important. The company cannot run without effective human resource processes to hire and train the best people. You cannot function without effective information systems, or financial systems. However, they are not what the customer is paying for unless, of course, you are an accounting firm, information systems firm or training company. Then these are core processes. Support or enabling processes may be critical processes if they are considered to be among the most essential to improving quality and competitiveness for this organization.

Defining the core process is essential so that the dog is wagging the tail and not the other way around. It is the core process that must achieve the strategy, not the enabling processes. On a visit to a manufacturer who later won the Malcolm Baldrige award we walked around the plant with the plant manager. He described his expectations for the Whole System Architecture we were about to start to facilitate. During the course of his explanation, he mentioned that we didn't need to worry about the information systems, he already had a team designing those. We asked, "You do want us to consider redesigning the way the work gets done and the organization of people, right?" "Oh, yes," he replied. We were to consider the entire process of work and organization, but they were already designing the information systems! Clearly, the tail was about to start wagging the dog. The structure of work and organization defines the inputs and outputs to the information systems and defines the information system requirements.

Step 3: Define the Current State

How is the work performed today? What is the current work process? Mapping the current processes helps people understand the whole work system and gives the design team a common starting point.

It may seem that the design team members who work daily within the current work process would all have the same understanding of the steps in that process. This is almost never the case. The members of the team will generally be expert only in parts of the process, not the whole process. Unless they understand how the parts of the process fit together as a whole, they do not have the basic information they need to analyze the process.

We have repeatedly seen that even managers responsible for large organizations are not aware of how the work flows through their organization. For example, in a major semiconductor company the department managers mapped out the current steps in the work process. One of the managers commented, "I have worked here for sixteen years, and the truth is that until we mapped out this process today, I didn't really understand how the work got done. In fact now that I see how it does get done, I am even more amazed that it gets done at all!" That reaction is typical.

There are four major types of maps that can be used to define the current state of the work process. One of the four, *picture mapping,* provides a macro picture of the total unit or organization to be analyzed. The other three mapping techniques are as follows: *state change mapping, process flow mapping*, and *relationship mapping*. These provide more detail about the "state" changes of inputs and outputs, work activities, and relationships between people, units and departments. They can be used separately or together to get a complete picture of the current technical systems.

Relationship Mapping

We have found relationship maps to be one of the most useful methods for studying the work process, at every level of the organization. The advantage of a relationship map is that it illustrates how the work flows among those who participate in the process. A relationship map may also be used to illustrate the flow of material or manufacturing work as well as information or decision-making work.

On the left side of the page, you write down all of the people or groups of people who participate in the process. Then map the flow from left to right in chronological order across the map, drawing arrows as the work flows.

It is a fact of life in today's corporation that we have devoted more attention to the design and management of entry-level work than we have to work done by our highest-paid employees. The work of managers and professional staffs has gone relatively unplanned despite the fact that this work has the greatest impact on customer satisfaction.

If as Dr. Deming has said, managers are responsible for the design of the system, managers are certainly responsible for the design of their own system of management work and decision-making. Most quality problems are system problems. Some of the worst work processes are those among managers and professionals.

Take a look at the following map of one work process of a management team. This team is the senior management team of a chemical company. The team is responsible for, among other things, managing research and development. This map describes how they currently function and how they redesigned their decision-making process. When you examine the current state map, realize that they have not planned the work this way. It just happens! It developed over time without any deliberation. This is typical behavior in a corporate culture. Work relationships just assumed patterns. They are the result of habits.

What principles are evident in the current state map? This management team applied the following two principles to their process analysis: 1) Maximum teamwork among the members; and 2) Maximum input from and responsiveness to customers. They also worked to reduce the cycle time of the process.

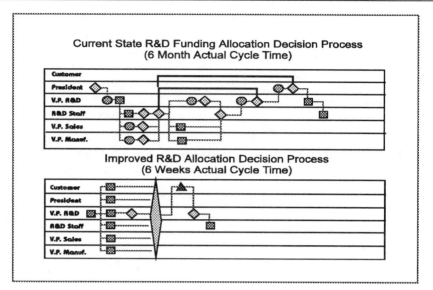

When the design team is mapping the current state of processes they may cover several walls of the their meeting room. Simply looking at the process map and thinking about the principles stated in the charter, principles such as "continuous flow", and "eliminate waste", or "make decisions at the lowest possible level" lead to obvious ideas as to how to improve the process. Look at the following map and imagine what problems it may reveal.

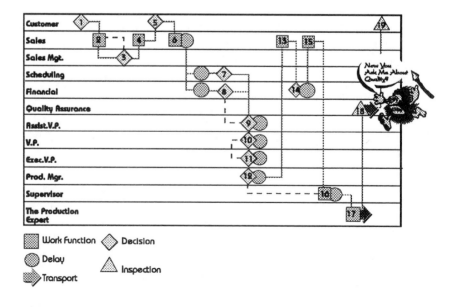

Step 4: Analyze the Processes

Once you have defined the current state, you have already begun the process of analysis. As we looked at the relationship maps for management decision-making process, questions became apparent and the sources of problems jumped out.

There are, however, a number of disciplined analysis approaches that will prove helpful in pinpointing problems and pointing to solutions. First, conduct a variance analysis to identify sources of problems. Look at where they occur, their cause, and the way they could be controlled. Second, analyze cycle times, and create an interruption-free process. Third, analyze the current state against your principles, vision, and values, and decide what changes are necessary to create conformance to those principles. We will not go into detail in this Leader's Guide. To explore these methods in greater detail refer to the *Change Management* workbook.

One type of analysis that is both non-traditional, and increasingly important, is the analysis of knowledge-work. One of the reasons so many improvement processes fail is that they do not recognize the unique nature of knowledge work, increasingly the majority and most important work in the modern corporation

Knowledge work is nonlinear and reflects a complex system. Complex systems, like the human body, weather patterns, and the free economy, may appear chaotic but are actually governed by transparent organizing principles. To understand, analyze, and design knowledge-based work and organizations, it is important to understand complex, nonlinear systems.

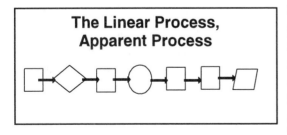

The Linear Process, Apparent Process

Let's start with a beehive. It is a perfectly ordered little corporation, incredibly efficient, reliable, hard-working, and designed to utilize its resources in the most efficient way. Frederick Taylor could do no better. And how is this order maintained? How are decisions made and executed? It was once believed that the queen bee sat atop a traditional hierarchy issuing decisions to be executed. This has been disproved, and we now know that the queen is a mere servant to the hive. The swarm of bees is able to make momentous decisions with no apparent hierarchy of decision-makers. Deciding to pack up and move, leave and create an entirely new hive, is a decision requiring the concurrent obedience of twenty to thirty thousand swarming workers - a good size corporation.

Kevin Kelly, an editor of *Wired Magazine* and a beekeeper himself, gives the following description of how a hive makes the momentous decision to abandon its hive and in a swarm move to a new location: "When a swarm pours itself out through the front slot of the hive, the queen bee can only follow. The queen's daughters manage the election of where and when the swarm should settle. A half-dozen anonymous workers scout ahead to check possible hive locations in hollow trees or wall cavities. They report back to the resting swarm by dancing on its contracting surface. During the report, the more theatrically a scout dances, the better the site she is championing. Deputy bees then check out the competing sites according to the intensity of the dances, and will concur with the scout by joining in the scout's twirling. That induces more followers to check out the lead prospects and join the ruckus when they return by leaping into the performance of their choice."[1]

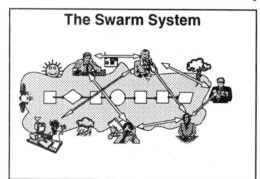

The Swarm System

Without order from above, order is created by the swarm. But it is not order created by the hierarchy of authority, decisions made, decisions executed, and measurement reported. Rather it is the order of patterns, laws, shapes, tendencies, or the transparent order of complex, non-hierarchical systems. The order is in the specific behavior and habits of the organization's members. When the queen is moved and the swarm follows, it does so in perfect unison. Each bee flaps its wings and emits an odor of rose from a gland under its wing. The odor is passed on to the worker behind saying, "the queen went this way, follow this way," and all thirty thousand give and receive the same message, one to the next. What a perfectly designed system, free of any

---

[1] 1 Kelly, Kevin. *Out of Control.* Reading, MA, Addison-Wesley Publishing Company, 1994. P. 7.

bureaucracy of central control and controllers, no home office accounting, performance evaluation, or reward systems!

When the transparent order of complex systems is understood, we accept and appreciate the natural order of things. One of the best examples of complex systems is the functioning of our own free economy, free of the hand of the engineer's order or Taylor's control, but subject to its own natural laws.

In the early days of the cold war thaw, Russian bureaucrats came to the United States and attempted to understand our system. They wanted to know "who decides who can start a new company?" And the answer that, "anyone who wants to," fell on disbelieving ears. "This is too important. Someone must approve this." "Who decides who gets how much capital? Which committee makes this decision?" The answer that anyone can give capital and anyone can ask others for capital again fell on disbelieving ears. To the mind programmed to expect predictable order, the chaos of a free economy contains too many inefficiencies and failures.

We are so conditioned to the free economy that we accept the inherent efficiency and transparent order of this nonlinear complex system. Knowledge-based work is very similar to this. The challenge is to understand the order; decide what parts of the process need to be shared, made public, and standardized; and decide what information, people, and tools are necessary to do the job most creatively and efficiently. This same thought process needs to be applied to the economy of information within the organization.

There are some additional tools to consider for analyzing nonlinear or knowledge work. Because information and knowledge are the raw materials and products of the process, the information system and information technology and practices are important to understand and match to the future organization and customer needs. Using the information flow map described in the workbook can help you identify the current information flow and what gaps hinder learning and need to be closed for the future state.

The keys to effective knowledge work are the correct generation, transfer, and utilization of knowledge. This involves people as well as technology, so there are critical people questions that must be addressed. The tool we recommend for this analysis is deliberation analysis. The term deliberation (or collaboration) is similar to decision-making. Deliberations are the series of discussions, exchanges, and considerations that take place prior to a decision. In the workbook you will find a number of forms and exercises for analyzing the deliberation process.

Step 5: Define Ideal Processes and Work Systems

There has been enough analysis! Now it is time to change things!

It is time to make decisions about how the process and work system can be improved. Of course many of the necessary changes have become obvious during the stages of analysis. While the design team is conducting this analysis, they should be keeping lists of ideas for improving the work system.

Designing the "ideal" is important when the design team begins to decide on their new process. There is a danger in being practical. If you are practical, suggestions for change will be met with, "Well, we can't do that because of this...". Usually this is because people are still thinking about the current way work is done or the present human systems. If the discussion about what can be improved is a "practical" discussion, it is likely that little or nothing can be changed. You must be impractical. Focus on the future. Focus on what is possible or probable in the future, not now. Design the ideal system. When you do this, you decide to change the whole system, and you make major leaps forward.

You will now re-map the process from the beginning. Begin where the input is received from suppliers, and review every step in the process. Do not worry about who will do what in the future state. Do not try to fix human systems. Just focus on the work system, work processes, technology, equipment, etc.

The design team should have the process and relationship maps on the walls of the meeting room, displaying the current system for easy and quick reference. They may also have lists of recommended changes based on their analysis. Now they should create a new map on the opposite wall, reorganizing the workflow and relationships. This will become the ideal state map.

Go through each step, and ask the following questions:

1. **How will we eliminate waste?** Any unnecessary step is waste. Anything standing or waiting is waste. Any time spent on unnecessary activities is wasted time. Eliminate everything that is not necessary.

2. **How can the process be changed to eliminate or control variances?** You have analyzed the causes of variance, and you have proposed solutions. Now design those into the new system.

3. **Can we change the process to increase individual learning?** Design work for intelligent people, and you will find you have intelligent people working. They will act intelligently when intelligence is called for. Provide information, feedback, and training to enable people to work smartly.

4. **How can we eliminate non-value-adding activity?** Are all of the steps in the process necessary? Could some be eliminated or combined for greater efficiency?

5. **How can we increase employee control and eliminate frustration?** Variances often occur because employees do not feel that it is their job to control quality or to change the process to achieve results. They have learned this from a system designed to minimize their input. Redesign the system to create control. When designing the social systems, you will create the incentives to motivate employees to control well.

6. **How can we eliminate interruptions?** A quality process is an interruption-free process.

Step 6: Analyze Cost/Benefits

Once the future work system is designed, the design team presents the completed analysis and recommendations to the steering team. The design team should realize that it has a responsibility to sell the new system to the steering committee. To sell simply means that the case must be convincing that the benefits will outweigh the costs, risk, and effort required to change to the new system.

Skepticism is a necessary and healthy attitude of science. In other words, if someone argues for a new idea, a new practice, a new way of thinking, the burden of proof rests with the proponent of the new way. Otherwise every new idea, no matter how wild and crazy, would be adopted and the old idea tossed out. This would lead to chaos! The steering committee is justified in saying, "Show me."

At this point in the transformation process, the design team, with help from the steering team, should do some preliminary cost/benefit analysis on the work system future design. A more complete cost/benefit analysis is done during implementation planning.

Step 7: Get Feedback on New Work System

The ideal state design is not finished at the end of the technical design. The next step will be to do a human systems analysis, then combine and align the business, work, and human systems into an optimized design.

The steering committee probably will need some time to discuss these questions among themselves. However, the longer it takes to decide the answers to these questions, the slower the redesign process becomes. One suggestion is to plan a day for the presentation and feedback process: four hours for the design team to present to the steering team, two to three hours for the steering team to meet by themselves, and an hour to give feedback to the design team.

One steering committee took two hours to agree to the answers to these questions; another took four weeks. If fast-cycle design time is wanted, steering committees need to decide quickly and efficiently.

Chapter Four
Designing the Human System

The human system includes how we hire, train, promote, develop, compensate, recognize, appraise, make decisions, and organize people. It includes the processes of managing people and decision-making. In short, it is the culture of the organization. In a world in which the work is less and less dependent on the mechanics and more

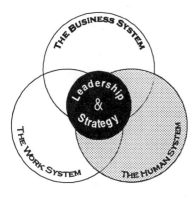

and more dependent on human competence and commitment, the human systems become more important. Reengineering the human systems is a high priority for most corporations.

Unifying the design of the work itself and the way people are managed is a major step forward. Too many people trying to change the culture of companies are divorced from the requirements of the work process. On the other hand, most efforts to improve the effectiveness of the work fail to deal with the essential tools of motivation and human development - training, compensation, recognition, and feedback systems. And most business strategy is divorced from both of the other systems.

Most organization redesign efforts are based on some macro theory of organization, forming the new organization around markets or geography, horizontally, vertically, or some other organizing principle. These reorganizations rarely improve real performance. Often the only work that is taken into account is the work of very senior managers who will manage a product group rather than a geographic region or vice versa. The work of the people actually talking to customers, designing, engineering, or making a product goes untouched. Many companies go through major reorganizations every few years and they have no impact where real people are doing real work. These reorganizations do, however, keep the executives distracted for another year, assuring that they are unlikely to pay attention to how real workers are doing real work that goes to real customers that pay real money. It is somewhat like in feudal times when royalty would marry, form alliances, and write treaties creating new structures, while the work of the peasants remained untouched and unchanged.

The most important work of the organization is the work along the core processes, those that serve customers and cause customers to write checks to the company. If the organization is to be designed to maximize performance to the customer, it makes common sense to begin the design of the organization at the bottom, where real people do real work. Doesn't it make sense to optimize the ability of first level employees and teams to improve their work, to think and make decisions about their work, to accept responsibility and pride in their work, and to link their work to the business performance of the organization? *Designing from the bottom-up, around the work, is a key principle of high performance organization design.*

Take a quick look at those companies who have been capturing market share, gaining value for their shareholders, and creating job security for their employees and you will find uniqueness of human systems. Southwest Airlines is a culture that regards every employee as a manager, owner, and full partner in the business, and the behavior of the CEO is in no way aristocratic and creates a common bond with those at the first level. The culture creates the key ingredient of high performance, first-level ownership and responsibility. Microsoft has a culture that puts the intellectual competence of the first-level and newly hired employees as a priority of the most senior managers. The most senior executives participate in the hiring of first level programmers because they know that the hiring decision is among the most important decisions made by the corporation. The work performed at the first level by "the world's greatest experts" has enabled Microsoft to become the dominant player in personal computing software. In both of these companies the executives know who does real work and what it takes to get the real work done. The system is designed around the real work.

James P. Womack and his associates at MIT spent five years and five million dollars studying the differences between auto assembly plants in the U.S., Japan, and Europe to identify the key differences in the systems that were the cause of different levels of quality and productivity. *"What are the truly important organizational features of a lean plant - the specific aspects of plant operations that account for up to half of the overall performance differences among plants across the world? The truly lean plant has two key organizational features: It transfers the maximum number of tasks and responsibilities to those workers actually adding value to the car on the line, and it has in place a system for detecting defects that quickly traces every problem, once discovered, to its ultimate cause....So in the end, it is the dynamic work team that emerges as the heart of the lean factory.* Even in the factory, where work is largely linear and definable as apparent processes, the key to high performance is the human system. In an organization in which the work is largely nonlinear and the process is more transparent, the key to high performance is even more so the human systems, or culture of the organization.

Behavior and Culture: The 5 "S" Drivers

Instead of simply listing the human systems, such as performance appraisal, compensation, and so forth, it will be useful to place them in a context in terms of how they influence performance in the organization. When considering the systems that drive human performance, the unit of measure that we are attempting to influence is behavior. When designing work processes effort is focused on cycle time, process steps, redo loops, and waste in the form of piles of delays. When considering the business system, the measures you focus on are revenue, expense, and asset utilization targets. Of course, there is a direct relationship between behavior and cycle time, revenue, and the other measures of the work process and business systems. However, it is useful to have a focal point when evaluating each system.

Culture is the sum of the habits of the members of the organization. Habits are behavior patterns that are automatic, requiring no external control. These habits develop, however, as a result of control or influence by outside forces. You have a habit of speech, your accent. You were not born with this accent, you were taught, and you learned as a result of models in your early environment. All habits are similar. They were developed from modeling and reinforcement. Our job is to study those habits that lead to operational effectiveness and design those influences that will strengthen those behaviors and increase the likelihood that these will become habits.

Habits that comprise the culture are not only the obvious and overt behaviors. They are also emotional and mental habits. One of the best and most clear observations in working with world class and mediocre companies is the difference in how people think. The world's best companies are, quite simply, smarter. The managers and employees think differently at Intel, Motorola, Corning, and Toyota than members of less successful organizations. Continuous improvement is not a program - it is a habit of thought and behavior. Quality is not a program - it is a passion and a thought process. A high performance organization is simply a smart company, one in which people study hard, learn well, and apply their learning quickly. How do superior companies become smarter? Of course, they may hire smarter people. But, more frequently, they develop the culture, the habits that lead to innovations and effectiveness.

What are the elements of the human system that you can design, change, and manage to improve the culture of your organization? This model, illustrated here, may be helpful. At the center is behavior, the habits that define the culture. There are five "S's" that can be designed,

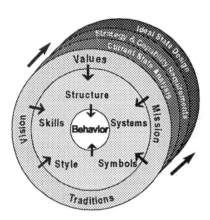

changed, and managed which are the major influences on the culture of the organization. Structure, Systems, Skills, Style, and Symbols comprise the human systems of the organization. Structure is how the individuals, the teams, the departments and divisions across the organization are grouped. This includes the levels, functions, or networks that make up vertical structure of responsibility. The systems include information gathering and distribution, feedback, compensation, appraisal, and any other activity that is carried out on a regular basis to influence human performance. The skills are the competencies, including technical and management or social. The style is the pattern of communication, the habits of sharing, trust, openness, and relationships. The symbols reinforce the values of the culture. Just like religions with their stars or crosses and tribal cultures with different dress, masks and face painting to designate status, corporations have their offices, furniture, parking places, clothing, and titles which reinforce what and who is important.

The Process of Human System Design

How then do you go about designing an entire organization and all of the systems of managing people? Where do you begin? Fortunately, the best place to begin is where you have already been. Design the work process, then design the organizational structure around and to support that work process. As discussed in the last chapter, it is best that a design team be chartered to do this work in a careful and thorough manner. It is important that the same design team that designed the work process also design the organization around that work process.

The following eight-step model for designing the human systems appears very orderly, beginning with principles and going through implementation. The presentation of this process is linear, going from step one, to step two, and so forth.

However, the reality of doing this design is a bit more nonlinear, complex, and interactive. The design team, during the course of designing the work process, has already identified many characteristics of the human system. When designing the structure of teams the design team will inevitably begin discussing training requirements and information system requirements. Later, when they get to a thorough discussion of these issues, they may make decisions that will cause them to go back and reconsider their original design of the team structure. This interactivity, or nonlinear design process, although sometimes frustrating is a requirement of designing the whole system. Every component of the system impacts every other component and it is impossible to prescribe one right order of consideration and decision-making.

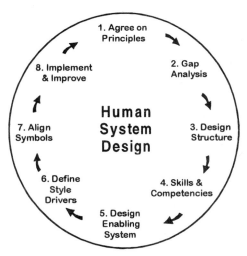

There are two kinds of principles with which you should be concerned. The first are general principles concerning the process of redesigning the human systems; then there are principles specific to your culture. If you are a rapidly growing high technology company, certain cultural principles are important to your organization and will be considered in shaping the human systems. A bank, a slow growth manufacturing firm, or a government agency would each consider different principles.

Principles of Human System Design

1. Design from the Bottom-Up and Around the Work: The only reason organizations exist is to facilitate the work. Customers pay for the products and services produced by the core processes. Design to optimize this work.

2. Minimize Walls, Divisions, Hand-offs, and Levels. Each of these represents an interruption in workflow and a possible source of variance.

3. Make Chairs, Not Legs. Pride and ownership come from completing a whole work process resulting in a complete product. Craftsman made complete chairs. Factory hourly workers were organized into leg, seat, back, and assembly departments. Pride, ownership, and quality were lost. Create teams and departments to increase intimacy and ownership.

4. Design Competencies for Future Performance: Organizations don't perform; people do. There is no such thing as a competent organization; there are only competent people. Different types of performance require different competencies and the design team must design the structure and systems to build required competencies.

5. Design for Continuous Learning: Design feedback loops and shared learning mechanisms to insure continuous improvement in work processes.

6. Create Models for Desired Behavior: People imitate the behavior of significant others. Habits cannot change at one level only. Design human systems and structures that must be practiced by all levels and reinforced by all systems. Design consequence systems as well as reinforcement systems.

7. Create Extended and Networked Intelligence: Create collective intelligence through formal and informal networks, interaction, and communication systems.

8. Reinforce Superior Performance: People perform when it matters. Make performance matter. Design the systems to recognize and reinforce superior performance. Design multiple systems of reinforcement.

9. Design around Both Process and Expertise: Design in ways to share and increase expertise, personal growth, and development.

10. Design Symbols to Reinforce Values and Behavior: Change necessary symbols to support the new culture, work system, and human system.

11. Changing the Structure Does Not Eliminate All of the Problems: The structure of the organization can only fix a fraction of the problem. The other social systems must be modified to support and balance with the work system, business system, and the business strategy to achieve full results.

Step 1. Agree on Your Cultural Principles

When our Founding Fathers met in Philadelphia to draft a new constitution, to design a new system, they had to first agree on common principles. Even with common principles they had vigorous debates on the structure and systems of the new country they were designing. Can you imagine if one of them had had in his mind the principle of theocratic rule, while another was seeking to finally create the proper monarchy, while a third believed in principles of pure Athenian democracy? There would be no possible way for them to reach consensus. Consensus requires common principles, common vision, and common understanding of the needs imposed by the environment.

Step 2. Gap Analysis

What is the gap between the current state and the ideal state? What is the difference between how we would ideally like to see people behave in the organization, compared to how people do behave today?

There must be a competency strategy. Companies win by doing things better, smarter, and faster than their competition, and these are all characteristics within the people as well as processes of the organization. But, smarter in what? You cannot be smarter in everything. The design team needs to review the definition of capabilities stated in the charter, understand them in the light of the company strategy, then define exactly what capabilities they will focus on developing to be a leader in their market.

General Electric is famous for Jack Welch's strategy of each business unit becoming number one or two in their markets. An antecedent to this strategy is to become the smartest competitor in a knowledge sector. In what areas are you going to be able to outsmart your competition? When you know the answer you can then design the systems and structure to achieve this goal.

For example, if the organization is a pharmaceutical research laboratory, the capability strategy will have specified capabilities to conduct research and discover new drugs in specific areas such as critical care, cardiology, or women's health. Processes and human competencies are required to be successful. The design team has designed the process and now will develop a *competence profile* for the organization. The competency profile will detail the specific competencies required in order to be successful in critical care drug discovery, for example. These competencies will include chemists, pharmacologists, doctors, statisticians, etc. The specific competency requirements have to be developed after the process is determined because the decision might be made, for example, to contract out certain research functions, rather than include them within the organization. This would alter the required competencies.

Step 3. Design the Structure

The structure of organizations appears to have a life of its own. It grows, consumes, fattens, and becomes increasingly tall and rigid with no necessary plan. Given time, every government and company will tend to develop bureaucratic organization, stifling creativity and flexibility. It is a reasonable theory that from time to time the organization must create its own revolution, to rethink its structure from the bottom up with a clean sheet of paper as if it were starting over. Perhaps this is the meaning of Jefferson's theory.

"I hold that a little rebellion, now and then, is a good thing, and as necessary in the political world as storms in the physical."
Thomas Jefferson

The culture of all business has changed to demand greater flexibility, fast rates of improvement, and high customer focus. This is impossible to achieve in a bureaucratic structure. AT&T, Procter and Gamble, Wal-Mart, Moody's Investor Services, Corning, Shell Oil, and dozens of other companies have changed their structure based on redefined vision and values. They have recognized that competitiveness results from a total and permanent culture change.

Power is an old fashioned word, but it is as real today as ever. There is the power to make decisions, the power derived from access to information, and the power to determine reward and punishment. If we are seeking to empower employees, to redefine the assumptions about who can make decisions, who possesses information, and who determines reward and punishment, we must redefine the structure of the organization.

The more layers of management in an organization, the less likely that those at the first level will be empowered to make significant decisions. Each layer draws decision-making authority and responsibility up and away from those with their hands on the real work. A culture of total quality is a culture of self-management in which employees are responsible for the quality of their work. The structure must facilitate this self-management.

The only legitimate justification for organization structure is to facilitate and enhance the work that serves the customer, the work at the first level.

The traditional structure of the corporation has been built on the assumption that it was the manager's job to define, measure, and control the work of employees and that employees were not to make significant decisions regarding their own work.

The structure of the organization is among the most obvious manifestations of the beliefs of management. The structure of the Catholic Church, the Roman Legions, and the British bureaucracy all reflect the values of those who created them and those who live within. Structure and behavior are constantly interacting to form the fabric of the mini-society we call a corporation.

Most organizations are designed from the top down. The president asks, "What help do I need to manage the company?" Here is where the problem of organization begins. In reality, the president does not need any help. He has not yet defined what work he is doing to serve customer requirements. How can he require help if he hasn't yet defined his own work?

The most important work of any organization is serving its customers. Most of this work is done by the first-level employees. This is where the design of the organization should begin. Each additional level of the organization must be justified by serving customers or helping those who serve customers.

When you design a house, you make assumptions about what is important to those who will live in the house. Will there be many or few bedrooms? Will there be rooms for large gatherings or small? Similarly when you design an organization, you make assumptions about what is most important, what will lead to quality, and what will lead to success for that organization.

The following illustration of the traditional organizational structure graphically portrays the value of control. It reflects the assumption that individuals, not groups, are responsible for performance. It is an essentially linear organization with straight lines connecting squares, all of which have four sides with clean

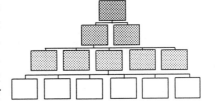

straight lines. It appeals to the linear mind in need of clarity and with low tolerance for ambiguity.

Teams can be formed over this traditional structure with each manager serving as the team leader. However, that does not dramatically change the relationships between team members and the manager. Another option is to assign more than one team to a manager. In many organizations a manager serves as the coordinator of more than one team. He may have three different teams with front-line employees as team leaders reporting to him and will, therefore, increasingly rely on their ability to manage their own work.

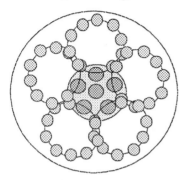 What values are reflected in the organization chart to the left? What behavior would you expect from people within such a structure versus within the traditional structure? Imagine that this structure is three, rather than two dimensional. Would that be more or less consistent with the reality of decision making and knowledge sharing in your organization? It is somewhat odd that by habit we draw organization charts with squares and straight lines, from top to bottom. Attempt to draw your own using circles. It is exactly this kind of thinking in which the design team must be engaged. There is not one "right" structure. There are only structures that, to a greater or lesser degree, promote behavior that leads to high performance.

Team Formation

The first task in creating the ideal structure is to optimize the effectiveness of the first-level structure, the work team. The following criteria should be considered when defining this structure. To decide how employees should be organized, you should consider how to optimize the following factors.

1. Team size: How large are families? How large are athletic teams? Groups seem to be able to work well together when they are of a typical size. Teams should be within the range of five to fifteen. There is a great deal of research on group decision-making and group dynamics that point to a range of eight to twelve as the best size.

2. Proximity: to work together in close communication and affiliation. We all possess the fundamental human need to group with others for common social purpose. We want to share responsibility with others. We want to be close to others. This is rooted in the need for shared protection, nurturing, and warmth. It is the basis of the family instinct. Families live within the same physical space. Similarly, teams function best when the members are situated close enough to rotate jobs, communicate, solve problems, train, and help each other when needed. The use of computer networks and team software support are changing this to some degree. However, face-to-face communication is still an important ingredient of group effectiveness.

3. Control: to control the process of one's work. Employees want to feel a sense of control. When one feels a lack of control, one feels helpless. Helplessness leads to lost motivation, slow work, and lack of commitment.

4. Customer Focus: to know one's customers, to listen and respond to the feedback and requirements of customers. Teams function best when they have a common focus on the same customer(s). Knowing and satisfying the requirements of *both* internal and external customers is the primary reason for the existence of the organization and ultimately the existence of the team.

5. Continuous Learning: to have the opportunity to expand one's abilities, to be challenged to grow and develop is intrinsically satisfying. The infant crawls to explore new territory, to gain new experience. This crawling never stops. People who are mentally healthy, energized, and happy are people who are in the process of learning and growth. They are challenged to develop themselves.

6. Ability to Solve Problems: to improve the process and exercise individual and collective intelligence. Employees want to be able to solve problems. A feeling of empowerment and motivation is derived from participation in problem solving. Employees can solve problems when they have common knowledge, have access to all the pertinent information, see the relationship of work activities and their effect on team performance, and give each other feedback.

7. Knowing the Score: to keep track of performance is essential to motivation. Feedback that is specific, immediate, and frequent increases the rate of response. The design of the team should take into account the ability to create scorekeeping. Form each team around a process that can be controlled by the performance of all team members. To improve their score and reach a common goal, the team must coordinate all team member's efforts.

8. Share Work and Help One Another: to be able to assist other members of the team and feel that one is contributing to the whole. When interdependent employees work together on the same product or task, they create a feeling of helpfulness which increases self-esteem. A lot of work is organized so employees work alone even though they may be on a team. Only when all members work together can the team succeed.

9. Eliminate Wasted Time, Effort, and Material: Design the team effort so that unnecessary tasks are eliminated and the process speed is optimized. When forming the team, one must consider time. It may be desirable to perform a whole process, but some elements of that process may reduce efficiency of time so that the cost exceeds the benefits.

10. Each Level of the Organization Must Add Value That is Unique. The first level of teams is responsible for managing the day-to-day work process. The next level is responsible for managing and coordinating the decision-making and process boundaries of teams. Their decisions affect the next quarter or several quarters. The top management team is concerned with the overall performance of the organization. They set the strategy and are responsible for changing the culture of the organization. Their decisions affect performance one or more years out.

Optimizing Team Performance

Now you have decided on the basic responsibility of your first-level teams. Have you given the teams all of the authority, responsibility, information, and training that will optimize their performance? Or have you assumed that managers will perform traditional management functions? If you have done the latter, you have *sub-optimized* the team's performance.

Many of the traditional management functions can be placed within the responsibility of the team. Assigning these responsibilities to team members increases the expectations, the responsibility, and self-esteem of team members. It reduces the need for additional managers, departments, and layers. It also optimizes the ability of the team to improve quality.

After considering all of the previous factors you will come to a point when you have given the team all of the responsibility it can handle. It is then time to ask the question, *"What help does the team need?"*

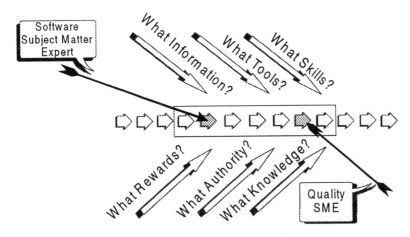

When you answer this question, you are beginning to define the roles and responsibilities of the first level of management or as we will call it **"Leader Level 1."** We suggest using this term to avoid creating confusion with current definitions of management or supervision. If you use the term "supervisor" or any other current title, the members of the design team are likely to fall back into the "village" assumptions about this role. Begin with a new or neutral title.

Ask two sets of questions. First, what functions should this person perform to assist the team and assure its performance? Second, what qualities and skills should this person possess? When you answer these two questions you are creating a job description for this role.

Once you have completed defining Leader Level 1 you will then group them into leader teams. They will also benefit from shared knowledge, experience and problem solving. How will this be facilitated? Who will facilitate this? Will this be done by a member of the leadership team as a "Subject Matter Expert," or will this be a second level of management?

It is very hard for managers (and all employees) to change their behavior. Redefining the position is essential to achieve this. If first-line supervisors in the old culture are simply assigned to lead a team, they are likely to assume their traditional behavior which will destroy the functioning of that team. Instead, they must be told that those jobs simply do not exist anymore. We now have a completely different job with different responsibilities, requiring different behavior. The unique value that the Leader Level 1 adds to the organization must be clearly defined.

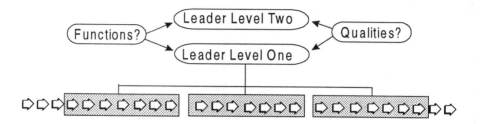

Teams in a manufacturing environment tend to do their work in a series of hand-offs from one team to the next. In a knowledge-work environment that may be still be true, but there are likely to be parallel teams doing similar work, perhaps in different regions, countries or focused on different markets. For example, a major software company will have software installation and service teams working in a city. They do essentially the same work done by parallel teams working in different cities. Forming these teams into a web can rapidly improve the learning and improvement process. Each team is finding better ways to perform their work and is encountering similar problems. Rather than hinder the flow of knowledge and experience with a formal chain of command, best to create an interactive web relationship that can optimize the ease of learning and sharing.

The nature of teams in a knowledge environment assumes a level of trust in the intentions and motivations of people not often assumed in traditional organizations. The complexity or chaos of nonlinear knowledge process and organizations will be thwarted by assumptions or needs for control. A recent and popular book by Francis Fukuyama[1] presents a well thought out argument regarding trust. *"One of the most important lessons we can learn from an examination of economic life is that a nation's well-being, as well as its ability to compete, is conditioned by a single, pervasive cultural characteristic: the level of trust inherent in the society."*[2] Fukuyama presents a detailed argument for individual virtues which are the bedrock of social relationships, or the tendency toward fluent association, what he calls spontaneous sociability. *"Spontaneous sociability is critical to economic life because virtually all economic activity is carried out by groups rather than individuals. Before wealth can be created, human beings have to learn to work*

---

[1] Fukuyama, Francis: *Trust: The Social Virtues & The Creation of Prosperity*, New York, The Free Press, 1995.

[2] Ibid., p. 7.

together, and if there is to be subsequent progress, new forms of organization have to be developed." The idea of social capital as a measure of wealth, the intellectual competencies and abilities of the members of society, has been presented before. However, Fukuyama directly relates social capital to the prevalence of trust in a society. High trust societies are more successful at wealth creation. Low trust societies demonstrate less ability to generate both social and material wealth. Low trust societies, such as in the Middle East and China, extend trust within, but little beyond the family association. Economic relationships are often within the family and those relationships beyond are treated with distrust. This is a brake on economic activity. High trust societies such as the U.S., Japan, and Great Britain develop multiple forms of association and ease of relationships beyond the family. These associations include the civic clubs, fraternities, political parties, trade and professional associations, as well as religious and other community organizations. This ability to "spontaneous sociability" is the foundation of economic activity.

What does this have to do with team formation and organization structure? We think of team formation as something that is designed one time and will be permanent. Perhaps a better model is a model of "spontaneous sociability."

Step 4. Defining Skills and Competencies

The design process must plan for all of the skills and knowledge necessary to meet the requirements of current customers and future customers. The design team must consider functional and technical skills as well as management skills.

The functional or technical skills of managers and employees have a generalized influence on the total culture of an organization. As companies mature, the definition of skills becomes less general and more specialized. The emphasis placed on the development of technical competence increases, and then as the culture slides toward decline, it decreases.

At the beginning of a civilization's life cycle, all soldiers make their own swords and shields. Primitive societies are low specialization societies. Soon specialization increases and there are sword and shield manufacturers. Before long each has separate departments of engineering, production, marketing, and research. With a continued dedication to specialization it is predictable that the coordination between these departments will soon break down, and they will pursue conflicting directions, wasting the energy and reducing the competitiveness of the organization.

Many of our modern bureaucratic organizations suffer the illnesses associated with over-specialization. This illness is common at the top and bottom. Executives at the top may know only finance and do not understand production or marketing. At the bottom the work is so fragmented that workers are unable to feel any sense of pride in a final product or service to a customer. The ideal synergistic model achieves a healthy balance between generalization and specialization in which high levels of competence are achieved, yet work is integrated and knowledge shared across specialties.

It is also likely that in the mature culture there will be a shift from the functional skills of product innovation, producing, and selling to the support skills of finance, planning, and personnel. The bulk of American industry in recent years has suffered from a shift in emphasis from the primary skills to support skills. Few graduate students are preparing for careers in manufacturing technology and management while a mass of MBA's are preparing themselves for careers in finance and strategic planning.

The design team should develop an initial team skills hierarchy. This hierarchy can be used in the development of a pay for skill/knowledge system or simply for the guidance of training and development efforts, which should be ongoing for team members.

This definition should include both **technical** and **people skills**. Technical skills should include operating equipment, specialized knowledge in mechanics, chemistry, sales, or any other function of the team. The people skills may also be called social or management skills. These would include training skills, team facilitation, problem solving, or any other skills relating to the ability of people to work together.

Step 5: Design Enabling Systems

Organizations maintain efficiency and sanity through dozens of systems: hiring, discipline, firing, communication, training, compensation, recognition, promotion, etc. Without systems every event would be treated as unique and require a separate judgment. Chaos would result.

What is the "order" the systems maintain? In a military organization all information flows upward to the commanding officer with little if any horizontal flow. The systems were consistent with the assumption that the officer made command decisions on the battlefield.

No one else possessed the information to make effective decisions. Undoubtedly for a military organization engaged in battle this system of information flow worked best.

Just as work systems were once largely linear, moving neatly in a straight line, human systems were also structured in a clear chain of command. And, just as work systems are increasingly nonlinear, and are web or "swarm" systems, so too are the human systems. Increasingly information within the organization is best shared in an interactive web, rather than in strict military order.

The systems of compensation and benefits in most organizations are based on the idea of societal classes, and they reinforce that idea. We assume that there is a vertical class structure requiring differentiation. Stock options are provided for senior managers but not for lower-level employees. Why? Obviously, we value managers at higher levels, more than front-line employees, and we want people to strive to move "upwards." Why not offer stock options for employees who progress laterally by developing more skills and improving performance within one layer of the structure? Do we not value such movement?

Similarly, profit sharing has traditionally been a system for the upper classes of our mini-society on the assumption that profit was controlled by the decision-making managers and not the employees who were merely following instruction, or doing their *labor*. Is that assumption still true? The existence of such a system teaches employees that they are not responsible for profit; their managers are. Therefore, why should they try to increase profits?

Every one of the systems in the organization is based on values and visions of the leaders of the organization. If you value the decisions of those at the first level, you will provide them information so they can make effective decisions. If you value their focus on the customer and on business performance you will provide reward or recognition for improving customer services and business results.

With each of the systems the design team will evaluate the current state and design the ideal state as they did with the technical systems. It may be useful to ask the following four questions for each system:

1. Who are the customers of this system?

2. What are the needs of each customer group for this system?

3. What characteristics should this system possess from the perspective of each customer group?

4. What enabling technologies can be employed to enhance this system?

If the design team has reached consensus on these four questions, it will lead toward consensus on the design of each of the systems.

The purpose of the design process is to optimize the organization's ability to anticipate and respond to its customers' requirements. Most current organizational systems were not designed with this purpose in mind. Using the environmental scan to evaluate the current systems, you may want to list pros and cons of each. Next, review your statement of principles (values) in your design charter. Then brainstorm ideas for an ideal system.

Knowledge Management System

Knowledge management has become a major focus of improvement in corporations today due to the increasing recognition that the quality and effectiveness of most work is dependent on the utilization of knowledge. The ability to access and utilize knowledge is a key component of the human system of the organization. [3]

Knowledge management is not simply creating knowledge within people – training and development, although that is one aspect of knowledge management. Knowledge management is also the creation of relevant databases and creating the fluid channels of access to data. *Knowledge management is optimizing the ability to accomplish business goals through the efficient use of knowledge.*

Many of the human systems impact knowledge management. Certainly training and development is a component. However, the entire information system and how it provides timely, relevant information, how it provides for interaction among knowledgeable individuals and how it is able to provide quick and user-friendly search functions are essential.

Step 6: Define Style

The character of day-to-day interactions among the members of an organization is that organization's style. Style is behavior, the specific behaviors of how we communicate and convey values, judgments, and priorities. The style of managers is inevitably linked to the struc-

---

[3] Also see "Teams and Technology" by Catherine M. Beise in *The Advanced Team Guide.*

ture and systems but also to their functional skills and even the physical environment in which the work takes place.

Style has a significant impact on the ability of an organization to make effective decisions, motivate its employees, and bring about unified action. The style of managers can be clearly viewed in the group decision-making process. One manager with whom we worked claimed to be a great advocate of participative decision- making. He said all the right things. In group meetings he would proclaim loudly that he wanted everyone to speak his mind and that, "This is a group decision." None of his managers were ever comfortable with or trusting of these proclamations. After observing his behavior or his style in the group, the reason for their disbelief was well founded. When he stated his view, he did so with an intimidating tone of voice that signaled to everyone in the room that there was only one right decision. When contrary views were stated, the very movement of his eyes made the mistake clear. His style dominated his own good intentions and stifled the participative process.

We worked in another organization in which the managers openly identified themselves as "gunslingers." They said some of them had "gunslinger eyes." Incredible as it may seem, they would sit around a table with their hands hidden under the table, would glare at each other, and the moment they caught someone saying something they disagreed with they would "draw." Their hand would quickly come out from under the table, point at the other person and say something like "what do you mean you..." They shot each other. Needless to say, this style did not encourage open communications or problem solving.

All of those habits and behavior that we regard as "people skills" and which become cultural norms in an organization comprise the organization's style. Today most companies have within their training department professionals who can present the elements of effective management style. However these training presentations unfortunately have little impact on behavior because they present a new style without changing the example provided by senior managers and peers. The behavior is one component of a culture, supported by the other Four S's.

Step 7: Align Symbols

We value our rational judgment and behavior. We look down upon other cultures with their rituals and symbolic gestures, dance, and clothing as something of the past. Yet, if we could see ourselves through the eyes of an archaeologist 1000 years hence, we might have quite a different perspective. Picking through the ruins of a once tall office building, our future archaeologist might find strange pieces of cloth tied around the necks of each male who was surrounded by other symbols of the decision-making class. He knew who was of that class because of their private offices, ritualistic in size and furnishing. He might attempt to develop a theory that the piece of cloth tied around the neck was used to signal approval or disapproval in the decision-making process. Perhaps he might theorize that it was slung over one shoulder to signal approval and the other to signal disapproval. Surely knowing what a rational society we had developed, he would assume that it possessed some functional value. Or would he look down upon us and assume that we were so irrational as to obey ritualistically customs to which we could ascribe no intelligent meaning?

We employ all sorts of symbols in ritualistic fashion, and like the inhabitants of other cultures give little thought to their origin or their impact on behavior. We have separate parking and entrances for managers. Why? Is it to send a message that managers are different, superior to, and more important than everyone else? Why do we want to send this message? The president of Honda America Manufacturing sits in his "office," a large room with dozens of other identical desks and with other employees all dressed like him, in a white smock-like uniform. Can he not afford a private office? Does he not understand that familiarity breeds contempt, and, therefore, he should not mingle so closely with his employees? Honda performs quite well despite this violation of the traditions of American corporate culture. Honda regards the principle of "Unity" and "Consensus" very seriously. They train their managers in these principles and have designed their culture to promote the spirit of unity and consensus.

Symbols are generally not important unto themselves. Whether the president of Honda has a private office or whether there are reserved parking places for managers has little impact on the bottom line of the company. It is the teaching impact of symbols that is important. It is the messages they communicate which changes behavior and impacts results. In the southern United States not too many years ago, there were separate water fountains for "White" and "Colored." The same water flowed into each so some said, "What's the big deal?" The importance of separate water fountains was the message of a culture that taught that the two classes and colors were not to mingle. Symbols communicate, and the communication was clear. The symbols had to be changed to change the process of learning and all the subsequent judgments and behavior that followed from that learning.

It has been our experience that changing symbols can be among the most powerful and important decisions a design team makes. While many perceive these as unimportant they communicate powerful messages of change to the organization. The greater population of employees is often looking for some symbolic changes to demonstrate a real change in the culture of the organization.

Alignment Check

When the design team has completed making decisions about symbols they have gone through all of the necessary steps in the design of the human systems. Because you have considered each of the human system components separately and separate from the work process it will be important to check the alignment of these elements. Consider this a reality check.

We suggest you look back at your work process. Go through each of the process steps and for each step ask, "How will our decisions about human systems impact this step and work process?" How will your new structure, compensation, feedback, symbols, etc. cause that step to be performed in the best possible way? If you are confident that you have designed the human systems to optimize the work processes you are ready to begin implementation planning.

Chapter Five

Competencies of Change Leaders

Some people believe it is easiest to be a leader when they have absolute authority and unchallenged control. They yearn for the certainty and simplicity of such an organization. However, it is the nature of mature cultures, either democratic countries or companies operating in the modern age of knowledge work and human capital, that the process of leadership requires far more subtle skills. The development of team based organizations and increased reliance on consensus decision-making does not diminish the need for individual leadership. Good leadership is still needed when there are well functioning systems and high employee involvement. These conditions only modify leadership requirements and necessitate higher level skills, particularly those that elicit commitment and creativity rather than conformity and compliance.

In order to create the future organization, designing the strategy, systems, and structure are not enough. To make the transformation possible and successful, leaders must develop new competencies. What are the competencies required? Following are nine critical ones.

1. Connective Thinking
2. Pursuing Worthy Purpose
3. Creative Dissatisfaction
4. Create Unity From Diversity
5. Think Globally
6. Exert Will
7. Systems Thinking
8. Build Consensus and Teamwork
9. Be Consistent and Trustworthy

1. Connective Thinking

The organizations of the future will require leaders who can think about the system as an organic whole and deal with the ambiguities and paradoxes presented by a dynamic environment. Balancing issues of productivity and quality, growing the organization with fewer people, understanding and integrating new technologies, and managing a diverse workforce are a few of these complexities. Different thought patterns are required than in the past. Certain thought patterns led to success in the era of family farms, others during the age of mass production, and yet others will lead to success in the 21st century awaiting us.

Kevin Locke is a Lakota Sioux hoop dancer from whom we can learn an important lesson about how we think and how we build organizations. Kevin said that the Lakota Sioux, when they first encountered the strange newcomers of European stock, gave them a name that seemed appropriate. They called them, "Oblatonyangpi," which means square people, or more literally, people of the square. Why? These immigrants carried many things that they would stare at for hours (books) that were all square. When they built their homes, the inevitably built squares which sometimes had additional squares within them. They cut out squares, windows, to view the world through. They hung squares on the walls (pictures). If they had a lot of houses, what did they do? They made blocks! Big squares. Strangest thing of all...they even tried to do square dancing! A virtual impossibility. Not surprisingly, the dancing was accompanied by someone obviously in charge and yelling down at those trying to do the impossible! Early supervision, perhaps.

How did the Lakota Sioux build houses? Round. When they had many houses, they formed a large circle. They sat and danced around the circle. Round people and square people. No wonder they had so much difficulty communicating.

Kevin Locke is a hoop dancer. The hoop or circle in Sioux culture is sacred. The finale of the hoop dance has the dancer holding a large hoop of hoops all connected in one great circle. It reflects the sacred prophecy of all the sheep in one fold and the unity of human beings with mother earth and father moon. The Native Americans understood connections, interdependence, and unity of the Great Being's creation. The Europeans understood straight lines, personal ownership, and separation or distinction between things. Those of European dissent loved private property and property lines that delineated "yours" and "mine."

This is the story of predominately linear and nonlinear thinking and habits. Our organizations are linear, yet the world is increasingly nonlinear. When we form organizations, we use boxes and straight lines. Why? Do they illustrate the reality of relationships or are they merely a cultural language with which we are comfortable? Our organizations assume clear and separate responsibility between marketing and manufacturing, engineering and human resources. They appear as clear boxes and straight lines on the organization chart. They are an illusion. The reality is one of shared responsibility and connected action. Success according to the bonus plan may be an individual achievement. But, success according to the customer and stockholder is a collective result.

The Native American was conquered by the advancing European mind because the Native Americans were in a state of harmony with their environment. They lacked the ability to combat the power of the linear processes that propelled the repeating rifle and railroad. Today, the linear process has reached the other shore and encountered its limits. It is confronted, not with the conquering of territory or laying of track, but with the productivity of ideas, webbed knowledge systems, and the necessity of bringing all associates into the circle of the business management process. The leader who is unable to create the unity of the circle will be conquered by a challenger who can.

2. Pursue Worthy Purpose

Two good pieces of advice for giving a speech are to be sure that what you are saying is important and be sure to let the audience know why you believe it is important. If it is not important, why are you wasting their time? If you don't believe it is important, you cannot convince the audience that it is important.

Delivering a speech is like the role of a leader in an organization. Leading is like standing in front of an audience. If you plan to lead people, lead them in a direction that is important. You must know what is important and be able to convey this importance to people. What can your organization accomplish that is important? What can the organization become that can make a difference, a significant contribution?

It is a human characteristic to seek meaning or purpose, a cause that is noble, or a focus for energy or sacrifice. The skilled leader helps people connect their lives, actions, and energies to that purpose. This is true in work organizations and in other aspects of life.

Both individuals and institutions who achieve excellence have a deep understanding of their purpose. This understanding of purpose is usually one that is uplifting, that creates within the individual a sense of self-worth and a reason to sacrifice and make a commitment. Many business institutions have lost their vitality because they focused excessively upon financial goals and measures and forgot their true purpose: to be of service to a customer and serve the needs of society by creating aggregate wealth. The objective of financial results, while necessary to the long term health of an organization, is not an adequate motivation for those who must perform the work of the organization.

Leaders create human energy by instilling a sense of purpose within their followers. The manager or administrator may direct and control the energy as the driver may steer and control the car. However, the car does not make progress without fuel in the tank or fire in the engine. It requires energy to make progress. Human energy is the fire that propels every organization forward toward its goals, and it is leadership that creates this energy.

The mystery of great leadership is the focus on a noble purpose and the willingness to call upon others to sacrifice for that which is noble. Every great leader has intuitively understood this process, yet it is sometimes lost in the day-to-day managing of the business. To lead the organization of the future, the purpose must be rediscovered and communicated to all.

3. Creative Dissatisfaction

I have rarely met an excellent executive who was satisfied, and I have known numerous mediocre ones who were. Those achieving excellence are participants in an ongoing struggle with their own competencies. They are active managers of their own learning process. This is similar to Andy Grove's (Intel's co-founder and CEO) paranoia which he promotes as a new management principle. Creative dissatisfaction is felt as self-criticism and an internal motivation to self-improvement, where Grove's paranoia is more a recognition of the challenges facing the corporation.

Change and progress occur as a response to dissatisfaction. If an individual is satisfied, then he or she stands still and has no reason to change or grow to become a closer approximation to his or her potential. Only out of dissatisfaction comes searching, discovery, change, and growth. Individuals who possess this quality of creative discomfort are those who are a work in progress. They are the most valuable commodity in an organization. They are able to adjust to change, to benefit from and to lead change. The ones who are satisfied are the inertia, the drag on an organization.

Leaders who want to help their organizations improve must look at themselves first. The ability to be self-critical, to welcome constructive feedback, and to manage one's own ego are competencies necessary for ongoing success.

4. Create Unity from Diversity

Organizational systems that promote or are built upon class distinction are the dinosaurs of our age. Corporations have preserved class structure through the distinctions between management and labor, salaried and hourly, and thinker and doer. They are all increasingly false and useless baggage, carried forward into a new world from a dying civilization. Class distinctions create a barrier to human development and block potential for both individual and institutional progress. Only through creating mechanisms of unity within the enterprise and recognizing the unity of the human race can the business thrive in the modern world. This is true in the organization's internal and external environment and relationships.

This is an age of disunity. It is an age of increasingly divided nations, races, religions, and political parties. It is an age where individuals seek self-promotion by highlighting their differences from one another. Yet, it is an age in which these differences are becoming increasingly transparent and irrelevant. This is an age of paradoxes. While there are increasing numbers of countries and increasing tribalism, these distinctions at the same time are becoming less and less relevant.

When the United Nations was founded in 1945, it had fifty-one member states. Today, that number is rapidly approaching two hundred. Futurist John Naisbitt in his book, *Global Paradox*, predicts that in the next century the number will approach one thousand. He states that, "A world of 1,000 countries is a metaphor for moving beyond the nation-state. Countries will become more and more irrelevant. The shift will be from 200 to 600 countries to a million 'hosts' of networks that are all tied together. The people we network with will become more important as the country we happen to operate out of becomes less important." The creation of a new world order is not a political philosophy or a position on the left or the right. It is simply a statement of fact, as the movement from agricultural to industrial societies was a material reality. The material of work in this new era is not farmland or industrial equipment; it is knowledge creation and management.

Leaders in the future will be those who can see unity and can bring people, ideas, and resources together in common purpose and understanding. The role of promoting unity and creating integration of knowledge is the key to leadership in the new age.

To be competitive and successful, organizations need to involve every individual in the process of management, problem solving, and decision-making. The reason is obvious: improved performance through unified effort toward a common goal. Competent leaders know this and work toward removing useless class distinctions and barriers.

5. Think Globally

Where are the borders of our system, the system that determines our competitiveness? Are they in a city, a region, or a country?

I recently found myself in Malaysia at a mountain top resort where I was leading a strategy retreat with my client, the UMW Corporation. As an American consultant I was struck by the realities of global integration sitting with the senior managers of this Malaysian company that assemble and market Japanese Toyota cars and Komatsu heavy equipment. The primary strategic issue for this company is responding to the challenge of the removal of trade barriers among Southeast Asian nations, the formation of the Asian Free Trade Association (AFTA) and the new role they will have to play on this more united stage. The managers are half Chinese and half Malay by ethnic background. We were eating dinner in a Korean restaurant while the music pouring too loudly from the stereo was the *House of the Rising Sun* (a New Orleans blues) sung by the British group the Animals. Communication was not a problem because English is the common language of all business in Southeast Asia and we easily swapped data files from my laptop to theirs in the common format of Windows 95. The client managers were all familiar with the up and down trends of reengineering and total quality management and were all well versed in the Toyota Production System, the globally accepted benchmark of effective manufacturing process.

This is the reality of global integration, and similar scenes are being repeated thousands of times every day. A common business culture is emerging; an integrated global economy is a fact. There is one integrated world economy. Although not complete in breadth or depth of integration, its momentum and acceptance is tantamount to its accomplishment. While it appears that there is an emergence of nationalism, there is a paradoxical dominance of globalism. The electronic currency of VISA and American Express care no more for the artificial boundaries of nation states than does acid rain or global warming. The Internet and the massive distribution of every kind of information, knows no national limitations. Capital moves from individuals to global mutual funds to corporations and back in seconds through fiber optic cable and satellite transmission with no concern for local currencies translated by computers. The satellite based transmissions of telephone, data, and television signals recognize no borders. Royal Dutch Shell, Ford, Honda, General Electric, and Sony not only are adept at leaping borders, but also create standards of price, communication, knowledge, and processes that are linking mechanisms of commerce through things and ideas.

The borders of the system within which most companies must be concerned are literally the borders of our world. In a previous era to be a multi-national corporation implied great size and power. Today, a small consulting firm may have a global network of partners and leverage its intellectual assets with no offices or physical property beyond its home office. The leader whose mind is confined to place is accepting an artificial boundary to his field of play. The system is global, and leaders must be able to deal with this.

6. Exert Will

Bulldogs. Determined. Persistent. Relentless. Show us a significant leader, and we will show you one of these characteristics. Creativity, vision, and good ideas are not enough to make change happen. It is the force of will that powers the muscle to achieve. Two individuals may have the same intelligence or vision, but entirely different forces of will.

The leader's ability to exert her will is the single most significant factor in organizational success or failure. Some executives casually desire to change their organizations. Others are in a fight for their lives and are willing to overcome all obstacles. One leader we know had a specific view of what he wanted his organization to be. He was the president and son of the original owner. Theoretically, he had the power to make his vision come true. But he was unable to overcome his natural reticence and desire for harmony. His direct reports had stronger wills and personalities and overwhelmed his vision with their own. Another leader with whom we worked did not take "no" as an answer. Through discussion, debate, prodding, and pushing, he was able to transform the organization's culture in spite of many naysayers.

Followers feel the will of their leader and the ensuing energy creates a collective will. It is the force of an army marching into battle in which the general desperately seeks to convey his confidence and determination to his soldiers because he knows that these qualities will confront and defeat his enemy. So, too is in business.

It is important to balance one's will with a leadership style that reinforces the type of change you are seeking. A Barbarian must know when to listen to others and when to be gentle. A Bureaucrat needs to be forceful and buck the system when it is necessary. Knowing and using the right style at the right time makes the leader great.

George Bernard Shaw said, "Reasonable men adapt themselves to their environment; unreasonable men try to adapt their environment to themselves. Thus all progress is the result of the efforts of unreasonable men." One might then say that all true leaders are unreasonable men because they believe in their ability to exert their will on their environment to create the future. Unfortunately, many never escape the control of the environment to assert their own vision, their own will. They have learned to be reasonable.

Leading a change process is an unreasonable process. In other words, it is not a response to immediate external demands; it is the creation of activity based on a vision of what could be rather than what currently is. The leadership team members must exert their will by imagining a future state, a strategic vision, for their organization. The change process is the drive toward that vision.

When Xerox went through their change process, David Kearns, then CEO, was very clear that the changes were not voluntary. Managers could adopt somewhat different courses, but they had to move in the direction strategy required. The same has been true at many companies that have succeeded in significant change. Their leaders have applied the force of will!

7. Be a Systems Thinker

Remember the movie, "Being There," in which Peter Sellers played Chancy Gardner, a somewhat simple-minded individual who had figured out the remarkable cycle of the seasons? Confronted with virtually any question, he replied that the winter would soon be followed by the spring when all would be renewed. Then summer, etc. Incredibly, some thought he was giving a brilliant dissertation on economics, and others thought this was an insightful political analysis. What he was doing was demonstrating the universality of a systems view, a recognition of cycles and patterns inherent in most systems.

Business is not quite as simple as the four seasons, although they both have similar cycles and cause and effect relationships. Too many business people do not recognize this fact, resulting in decisions made and actions taken in response to a singular incident or piece of data. Dr. Deming taught some of this when talking about statistical process control, the nature of work systems, and common and special causation.

Dr. Deming did not provide a model and method to analyze the larger system of the organization and redesign that system to reduce the causes of variation. Whole System Architecture is that model and method.

Peter Senge in the book *The Fifth Discipline* presented a primer on systems thinking and the relationship between learning and the operation of the organization's system. He discussed the circle diagram with a first cause, producing an effect that becomes a second cause, which affects a third, and then closes the loop by affecting the original cause. For example, training employees in the team process results in increased acceptance of responsibility. This sense of responsibility in turns, leads them to request, even demand, more information. This causes a need to redesign information systems. This leads to other consequences on other systems.

The effect of one system is rarely contained. It often produces consequences that may be either desirable or undesirable. This relationship between the performance of one system leading to the operation of another can proceed through hundreds or thousands of apparently independent systems. Imagine drawing the relationship between the development of the personal computer and cascading the effect from organization to organization. It is nearly endless. This is precisely how the larger ecological systems work with the progress of one species (one system) impacting a series of other species, together comprising the larger ecological system.

This is how the free economy works. There are an endless series of causal events with internal feedback loops that also impact secondary systems in a series. Within the corporation, there are similar interdependent systems. It is not too hard to imagine how one company system impacts the behavior of parallel systems such as competitors. Once a competitor sees you have made an adjustment in your work process or human system that produced superior business results, new behavior is triggered in the competitor's system. This is how the impact of increased import of Japanese cars triggered major alteration in automotive design and manufacturing in every automotive company worldwide.

Systems thinking is not difficult. Once you get the basic idea, you can apply systems thinking to virtually any field of activity. Once you see the systemic nature of things, it changes the way you see the world and the organization. The competent leader helps all members of the organization understand the workings of the system and participate in its analysis and correction.

8. Building Consensus and Teamwork

The organizations that succeed in the future will be those that are best at bringing people together and calling upon the input and participation of all. This requires a collaborative culture that uses consensus more than command. In the past, a leader would command his ship in battle, command his followers to order, and command his will upon his government. Our culture has emerged from a history that valued the strength of command. Command decision-making, shaped by the necessities of war, led to success on the battlefield. Organizations are not battlefields; therefore, command is not as necessary.

The institutions of the future will succeed because of their members' quality of thinking. Thinking is not something you can command. You cannot stand over someone, yell "think," and expect better ideas to emerge. Better ideas emerge when individuals feel that their ideas will be listened to, discussed, appreciated, and taken into consideration in an honest and open fashion. This is the style that stimulates creative thinking. Creative thinking is the most productive behavior in today's organization.

The leaders of the new era will be ones who possesses the skills and discipline to work with groups in reaching consensus. Consensus is best used on matters that are important to the business and would be improved by full team participation. Through consensus, the group with total candor arrives at a collective wisdom. A leader in this type of organization requires new skills and personal qualities. Rather than the strength of argument, the strength of asking questions and effective listening will distinguish the leader.

9. Be Consistent and Trustworthy

This is an age of distrust. We have learned that presidents lie, that corporations cheat, that lawyers seek to distort and deceive, and that clergymen live dual lives. The effect of distrust is disunity and apathy. If one cannot trust sources of authority, then one is left to wander alone, constantly apprehensive of others. This state is destructive for the individual and detracts from the progress of the organization.

To be a leader requires followers, and following is an act of trust. If one person is going to respond and arise to the words or actions of another, the individual must first trust the sincerity, integrity, and truthfulness of the first person. Any seed of doubt or distrust weakens the ability of one individual to influence another. All sound relationships, in marriage, business, or religions, are built on trust.

This principle is defeated in subtle ways. We can communicate to influence without being fully honest. The salesman may present his product to appear to be the best, cheapest, highest quality, or most superior product while knowing otherwise. The manager may fail to tell the employee the whole truth about where he or she stands. The executive may state that there are no more layoffs planned; and within six months, more employees are experiencing the trauma of layoffs. Unfortunately, perceptions determine the bond of integrity that holds individuals and organizations together. These perceptions are often unfair. The executive may have told the absolute truth when he stated confidently that there were not more layoffs planned. It was several months later that they were planned. The perception of deceit is still there. Avoiding these perceptions is not easy in an age when people have been trained by the media to seek out any hint of falsehood on the part of the leader.

These ten competencies are surely not the only ones required of the modern corporate leader. Knowledge of technology, finance, law and the political systems that impact the organization are all additional requirements. However, from a personal leadership perspective, these ten stand out as personal characteristics of leaders of high performing organizations.

Chapter Six

Leading Strategic Transformation

Beyond the ten competencies we covered in the previous chapter, there are actions leaders should take to ensure successful transformation of their organizations. Hold yourself accountable for doing the following things to support the transformation process.

1. Adopt the Right Time Horizon
2. Be Proactive
3. Integrate Change and Business Strategy
4. Do Competitive Benchmarking
5. Model Teamwork and Problem Solving
6. Reinforce Continuous Improvement
7. Perform Value-Adding Work

1. Adopt the Right Time Horizon

One of the most important habits for managers is the mental habit of thinking in the short or long term. It is common for managers to continue to manage with a short-range view when a long-range view is more appropriate for their level of responsibility. They have not defined, or adjusted to, the "value-adding" work that can and needs to be contributed at their level. We have worked with many senior management teams who have difficulty finding time for developing strategy, yet spend all their time on immediate operational issues that would be better delegated. They are tampering in the work of those below and failing to do their own work.

The first-level employee operating equipment and producing a product is highly focused on the present activity and is necessarily making immediate and short-term decisions. The employee may spend one hour a week in a team meeting examining the results of the recent past (weeks or months) and discussing how to improve the team's work in the short-term future.

Managers at the first and second level above the actual work spend less time focused on the present and expand their horizon in the direction of both the past and future. They have numbers that illustrate the results and effects of changes over the past several months and will have one-year goals.

Senior managers should spend little time on the present (unless there is a genuine crisis), some time on learning from the past, and most of their time focused on creating the long-term future. The higher managers rise, the less able they are to influence the present. The present is literally out of their control. If they are controlling the present, then they are doing the work of their subordinates. They are probably tampering with the work of middle and lower-level managers.

Because most senior-level managers are most comfortable dealing with the short-term, they tend to want culture change to happen overnight. Their expectations are often unrealistic regarding how long it will take to design and implement a significant change in their organization. Continuous improvement gains, operational improvements in the current system, can happen in three to six months, but it is rare that a strategic change in the culture and system of the organization will happen in six to twelve months. Two to five years is a more realistic horizon.

Constantly changing course and the failure to follow through are the most destructive behaviors leaders exhibit. One of Dr. Deming's Fourteen Points was "constancy of purpose." By this he meant that if management is to achieve world class quality standards, management must define its mission and course and pursue that course with constancy, without appearing to change course with each new financial report.

Changing the culture of an organization will normally take between two and five years. Leaders need to be realistic and pursue significant change, rather than short term change.

2. Be Proactive

Lower-level managers tend to be predominantly reactive. Machines break down, and they must react. Customers place orders and they react. Customers change requirements, and they react. At lower levels of the organization, it is necessary to react to external influences at a high frequency.

As one rises in the organization, one's time should be freed from the need to react to frequent events. If you are always reacting, your behavior is determined by others. In a sense you are a victim of circumstance. As you rise in the organization, you should achieve increasing self-control and self-determination. Those who make significant improvements, who lead, are not merely reacting. They are proactive. They are creating their future by exerting their will and determining the future of their organization.

The manager who is entirely reactive has in a very real sense no free-will. He is controlled by others. Those who are proactive are exerting their will on their environment. Virtually all significant change is the result of individuals who rise above circumstance, have a vision of the future, and exert their will to create that future.

3. Integrate Change and Business Strategy

Most improvement efforts are focused on short-term performance. For example, the quality profession has for the most part emerged from the factory. The focus was on reducing variability or defects within the current specifications or requirements. The statistical approach to quality has undeniable value in enhancing quality within the focus of current performance. Future performance will likely require entirely different specifications, products, services, and capabilities. Reengineering processes will typically seek to reduce cycle time and eliminate waste from processes to meet current cost requirements.

All of these efforts, while commendable, may be irrelevant to strategy. A strategic approach to change builds the elements of quality, organization, and processes based on the requirements of the future market and business environment. Future competitiveness is the focus of Whole System Architecture.

Change efforts that are tied to strategy are defined around the future customer's needs and establish the internal organization and capabilities that will meet these requirements. That strategy will include defining the technologies, human competencies, organizational structure, and systems that will result in future success.

4. Manage Competitive Benchmarking

What does it mean to be "world class?"

It means that every function, process, product or service is as good as, or better than, that of any competitive organization. World class cannot be achieved by focusing on the product or the output of the system alone. The best product or service in the market today is already out of date if its producer is already working on the next generation product or service. It is the next generation against which you must compete. It is the ability to create the next generation that is the key to competition. If a competitor has developed a system of product development, training, manufacturing, or marketing that is superior that system will soon produce a new product or service that exceeds their own product that was considered world class yesterday. The only way to compete successfully in product and service is to compete in process and systems.

It is the purpose of competitive benchmarking to identify world-class standards, to compare yourself against those world-class standards, and to set goals and action plans to exceed those standards. The goals should be considered in the process of design. The organization should be designed to achieve goals that exceed the current benchmarks.

Competitive benchmarking is a strategic goal-setting process. It is not intended to establish goals to be met this year. It is not a onetime process or an exercise to generate activity and then to be forgotten. It is better not to enter the process of competitive benchmarking unless it is understood as a long-term commitment to achieving world-class standards, self-evaluation, and strategic goal setting.

The competitive benchmarking process was acknowledged as one of the keys to the success of Xerox in recapturing market share reviving the company.

What are the benefits of competitive benchmarking?

- Benchmarking is a stimulus to continuous improvement. The four-minute mile for years seemed an impossible achievement. Once it was achieved by one competitor, it became an almost routine standard. If an industry standard has been a five-day cycle to process and fulfill orders and one competitor develops a way to fulfill orders in twenty-four hours, this will quickly become the new industry "benchmark" if the competitors have knowledge of the new standard. If they lack this knowledge, they will be at a blind competitive disadvantage.

- The ongoing process of benchmarking reveals not only the best practices but the rate of competitor improvement. Benchmarking will provide strategic information about the need for research and development, training, and other processes that are critical to maintaining a competitive position.

- Benchmarking will reveal competitive intelligence that will point to specific changes that are resulting in an advantage for your competitors.

- Motivation is increased by defining specific challenges, by the ability to see scores that indicate improvement, and by receiving recognition when goals are met. All of these should be incorporated in the benchmarking process.

- Benchmarking gives the leaders a strategic understanding of where they stand versus their competitors. It defines how great the gap is.

It is vital that leaders be part of the benchmarking process. They must get out of their offices to see what other organizations are doing.

5. Model Teamwork and Problem Solving

It is leadership's burden to be the example and to lead. It is the first and most powerful meaning of leadership. The leader who asks others to follow the course that he himself is unwilling to follow is no leader at all.

More than once we have seen management support a culture change below them, yet fail completely to embrace the practices themselves. This inevitably results in failure of the effort.

We have implemented total team systems throughout the entire exploration and production organizations of three major oil companies. In all three cases we trained and coached the very most senior team of managers to practice the teamwork, customer focus, and process improvement which they had prescribed for the entire organization. In all three cases employees below were very sensitive to the behavior of the senior managers, and the changes in their practices established the credibility of the entire process.

There has been a great deal written about teams in organizations. While every movement has its excesses and unwise application, the fundamental idea of management and employee groups leading to work effectively in teams, to share important decisions, to share learning, and to improve the quality of their shared processes, is an absolutely valid and proven process. Don't be deterred by Dilbert and Dogbert – teams work!

The senior team must be willing to work on its own practice of effective team decision-making, customer focus, process improvement, and other management practices if they expect these to become the norm in the organization below them.

As consultants working with many organizations attempting to make these changes, we have concluded that one of the most common reasons for failure is that the senior managers have accepted the new practices intellectually but not in their heart or their habits. They have not internalized the concepts because they have not practiced or seen their effect first-hand or witnessed their results. Their faith has not been confirmed by deeds, and it is only through deeds that their faith will become real. Without this strength, with the first pressures they quickly resort to their old style.

The solution to this is for the steering committee to be out in front. When the design teams are assigned and begin their training in the design process, the steering committee should begin training in the practices of team management and put those practices to work within their own team. This will include defining their own customers and processes, improving their decision-making, and developing a balanced business scorecard.

Some managers will immediately react that this sounds like a lot of extra work. However this is their work. It is not "extra" work. Making effective decisions, serving their customers well, etc., is the substance of their work.

6. Reinforce Continuous Improvement

One of Dr. Deming's Fourteen Points is "drive out fear." A high performing organization is one in which its members take initiative. Initiative, no matter how minor, involves the risk of rejection and failure. Fear is the enemy of initiative, and fear is the direct product of punishment.

Parents who punish often and reward rarely produce children who are unlikely to take initiative in positive directions but are highly likely to rebel and seek means of avoiding punishment. Similarly managers who punish often and reward rarely will not lead a high-performance organization. Rather they will produce fear and drive out improvement.

We have observed the effect of fear at every level of the organization. We have seen senior managers who would not pursue a strategy of business growth because previous managers who pursued growth ended their careers in disgrace by making bad judgments. The mere suggestion of a growth strategy produced visible anxiety in this manager despite a rather obvious need for a growth strategy.

There are only two ways to reduce fear while increasing performance: reduce punishment and increase reinforcement.

The problem with punishment is that it does effectively reduce the rate of a response. However it does not encourage a replacement. It does not teach positive behavior. If the teaching of positive behavior is absent, the only result is fear and avoidance. Leaders by their very position have a powerful ability to reinforce desired performance. The recognition, attention, and approval of senior managers can have a powerful and positive effect.

Managers at all levels must practice behavior analysis. This simply means that they must define the behavior which they wish to increase. For example, they may wish to increase the behavior of identifying cost-saving opportunities and take initiative on these opportunities. If they seriously want to increase this response, they have the responsibility to reinforce the response when it occurs. Someone in the past months has engaged in this behavior. By reinforcing the behavior, he will increase the probability or strength of the response.

Whenever a manager or management team says, "I wish people would...." the first analysis should be, "Have you reinforced this behavior when it occurred?" If you have not provided reinforcement, then you can understand why you are "wishing" rather than observing the behavior.

It is useful to understand that all behavior is influenced by the balance of consequences. For every behavior there is potential reinforcement and potential punishment. Something good or something bad may happen as a consequence to the behavior. The balance often goes something like this: "If I work late and get the report done by tomorrow morning, my manager may be pleased. However, I will miss my son's soccer game." Or, "If I suggest my idea for cost savings, my manager may appreciate the suggestion, or he may react as if it is a stupid idea!"

In order to increase a performance, it is not necessary to eliminate all possible fears. A slight shift in the perceived balance of consequences may be sufficient to increase the rate of response.

Much of corporate management is still dominated by a "macho" notion of toughness. The macho logic is often expressed as, "They shouldn't need to be patted on the head; it's their job to make improvements." Or, "A little fear didn't stop me from making suggestions. If they aren't strong enough to stand up for their ideas then they shouldn't be working here!"

We need more models in the corporation of real "tough men" or women. They should be tough enough to express their appreciation. They should be tough enough to go out of their way to understand the pains and concerns of their subordinates. They should be tough enough to overcome their own fears that inhibit them from recognizing the heroes below them.

7. Perform Value-adding Work

The process of Whole System Architecture involves defining the true value-adding work done by the organization. Value-adding work should be optimized and the organizational structure and systems designed to support this work. On the other hand, work that does not add value should be eliminated. Non-value-adding work is waste. The elimination of waste is a key process in creating a high value organization.

Waste exists at every level and in every function. Employees rework, restudy, replan, and redo. If the work had been done right the first time, it would not need to be "redone."

Managers and executives also do non-value-adding work which is waste. Managers spend hours discussing a topic in a meeting and then two months later are having the same discussion as if the first one had never taken place. This is waste. Managers have to approve decisions of subordinates when they do not have any value-adding knowledge to contribute to the decision. The decision may sit on their desk for days or weeks, adding cycle time, slowing the process, and increasing waste throughout the system. Managers spend time reading reports that contribute nothing to their own work. All of this waste should be eliminated.

All management team members should consider why they really exist. What is the essence of their management purpose? What would happen if they were eliminated tomorrow? Which of their activities would truly be missed by the organization or the customer? In other words how do they really add value?

We have consulted with managers who had great trouble answering these questions and realized that they spent the majority of their time engaged in waste. They realized how they had been robbed of the opportunity to do things that really called upon their higher talents and abilities. The energy and self-esteem of managers is often lowered by the requirements to engage in wasteful activity. Here are some typical value-adding and typical non-value-adding senior management activities.

High Value-Adding Activity

Strategic Analysis and Planning
Management of Strategic Implementation
Long-Term Financial Planning
Analyzing Strategic Technical and Human Capabilities
Recognizing and Encouraging Improvement Activities
Communicating with Key Clients

Typical Low Value-Adding Activity

Short-term Financial Reviews
Short-term Operational Decisions
Reviewing the Decisions of Subordinates
Reworking, Restudying Operating Plans

It often appears that everything is important to senior managers. The best managers have the ability to discriminate between that which is their value adding contribution to the organization and that best delegated.

Chapter Seven

Style and Strategy

There is no one right leadership style. The longer one spends studying successful organizations and their leaders, the more one is struck by the diversity of leadership style. There is a common thread among successful leaders. Style matches strategy. The style of the leader is linked to the behavior required of employees and the strategic response to the environment. In other words, an industrial chemical company experiencing slow changes in its market environment, will best be led by a leader with one style. A fast paced technology company, competing in an environment of rapid market changes will require different behavior on the part of employees and a very different style on the part of the leader.

The leader who is successful starting a new company is often a failure when a company is mature and complex. Different competencies and styles are required. Ross Perot was enormously successful as an entrepreneur and has been unable to cope with a complex organization with diverse and competing interests. The founders of Apple Computer, Steven Wozniak and Stephen Jobs, are modern heroes of an entrepreneurial age and industry. Both were not able to, or lacked interest in, managing a mature and diverse company. This should in no way tarnish their tremendous accomplishments. The late Robert Goizueta, CEO of Coca-Cola, was not an entrepreneur, had not had the creative energy to start a new company, and had not pioneered a new industry. He did, however, a remarkable job of building the value of the Coca-Cola company, expanding its markets, and consolidating its position as the leader in the beverage market world-wide. His style was different than a true entrepreneur and matched what was needed to lead Coca-Cola.

The Styles of Leaders

Many books have been written on the situational nature of leadership. One, which I wrote a few years ago, is *Barbarians to Bureaucrats: Corporate Life Cycle Strategies*. The book defines different leadership styles and their relationship to stages of an organization's life cycle.

The Prophet: The Prophet is the true visionary, creative leader who lives in the world of ideas. Thomas Edison was a terrible administrator but a creative genius. Steve Wozniak was the creative genius of the Apple II but did not have any organizational or administrative skills. The Prophet has great creativity and great faith in his ideas. He inspires faith and enthusiasm for his mission. Many companies are started by prophets who later fail when they try to lead the company to more mature stages of development. In the age of the Prophet, there is a usually a group of disciples or a band of followers rather than an organization.

In history, every civilization is accompanied by a great religion. We call many of the civilizations by the name of the religion – the Islamic or Hindu civilization. The "Word" was in the beginning. The "Word" is the idea, the vision that creates the motivation upon which everything else is built. Similarly, in companies, in the beginning there is the "word", the idea or vision, articulated by the Prophet and upon which the company is built. When the idea is lost the creativity is gone. One of the great challenges is to avoid crucifying and exiling Prophets to maintain the creativity in the latter days.

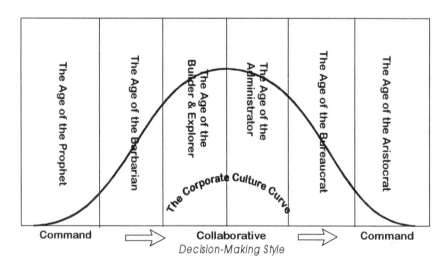

The Barbarian: This is the true heroic leader, like Alexander the Great, General Patton, or Hernan Cortez whose first order upon landing on the shore of Mexico was to burn the ships, leaving no doubt as to their direction. He is commanding, confident, and single-minded. This is exactly the type of leader needed in times of crisis and combat. Neither a consensus manager nor one able to deal with complex constituencies, this leader is likely to conquer territory then becomes a problem as the organization changes. Specialization, complexity, and diverse opinions do not match with his or her temperament.

The Barbarian is intimate with the work and the workers. Alexander lived for and loved the army, suffering with them, first into battle and first to take comfort, refusing drink when they could not drink, always sharing their pain. He made heroes of the common soldier, not the generals, because he knew who, in battle held the line – the image in the mind of the soldier of the heroic Greek soldier. He knelt with them and prayed after the battle and recognized their individual efforts. Ray Kroc, loved to flip hamburgers, visit the stores, and personally greet the employees. As Chairman of the Board, with thousands of stores, Ray Kroc spend half his time out in the stores. When he first visited the restaurant he would go to the restroom, like most customers, and if the restroom was dirty, he would get the bucket and mop, and personally clean it. If you are store manager and the Chairman comes to your store and starts cleaning your restroom it will leave an impression. Call him crazy if you will, but he did build a great company, largely through the establishment of values demonstrated by his personal behavior. Like most great companies, McDonald's was built on simple ideas: Clean, Quick and Courteous. The Chairman knew what was important and made sure everyone else did the same. This is the Barbarian.

The Builder and Explorer: These leaders represent the necessary specialization and differentiation in an organization as it grows and matures. The Builder builds departments, functions, and the mechanisms of production, while the Explorer expands territories and markets. Divisions between marketing and production and the development of other specialized functions arise under Builders and Explorers. These leaders are the technical experts promoting knowledge and technical skills. Magellan explored oceans with technical genius as well as courage and considerable political skills. Singular, command decision-making becomes dysfunctional as different interests, specialized skills, or functions need to be consulted and coordinated. Now in the cycle, whether in the progress of civilizations or companies, democratic forms of decision-making emerge.

The Administrator: Administrative functions are initiated during the reign of the Barbarian. As the organization becomes more complex, the leader increasingly must rely on those who do the counting and recording, the Administrators. Because of their function, Administrators have a natural desire for order and neatness and are troubled by actions that are not planned in detail. As Administrators become more dominant in the culture, the organization becomes more cautious, less likely to take risks or make very significant change. The predominant response to challenges from the environment are cautious and lack bold commitment.

The Bureaucrat: The Bureaucrat is the Administrator in charge, free to impose control and meet his needs for order. Those who violate the need for control are in trouble and likely to be punished or exiled. The Bureaucrat increasingly imposes mechanisms of control thereby stifling the creative impulse, assuring the organization is unable to arise to a new challenge imposed by the environment.

The Aristocrat: High in the organizational tower, the Aristocratic leader, wrapped in the trappings of wealth he inherited, is alienated and aloof from those who do productive work in the organization. Lacking empathy, the Aristocrat's actions have increasingly damaging consequences to those within the organization. He becomes more ineffective due to his lack of knowledge beyond his own advisors. Revolution usually follows as people recognize that their leaders are out of touch with their people and the challenges facing the culture.

The progression from birth to death, from Prophet to Aristocrat can be illustrated on the life cycle curve. Arnold Toynbee's, A Study of History (1962), analyzed the rise and fall of twenty-one civilizations and found that all cultures followed this similar pattern from birth to death. He also found the signal event in the decline of the culture was the failure of leaders to respond creatively to challenges. The creative response to challenges imposed by the environment is the mechanism of growth in the culture. Much like a muscle, the mind develops by exercising and responding to challenge. So too, does the culture of nations, civilizations or organizations progress by responding creatively to challenges imposed by their environment. The organization can be flexing and strengthening as the culture ascends the curve. Or it can be in decline and in increasing danger of being overcome by new Barbarians emerging in the environment. They are likely to be overcome if they have achieved what Arnold Toynbee called "a condition of ease." It can be argued that the economy of the United States during the nineteen fifties and sixties was so dominant and with so little worthy competition that it achieved a condition of ease. Surely this is true of the automobile companies who were soon to be challenged by the aggressive Barbarians of Honda and Toyota.

Toynbee concluded that civilizations were not defeated at the hand of external Barbarians, but were defeated internally by the loss of will, the loss of self-determination. Similarly, companies are more likely defeated by their own failure of strategy, failure to recognize and respond appropriately to the challenges of their environment. This is the ultimate failure of leadership.

The previous illustration depicts the life cycle curve of a culture, the typical type of leader, and the predominant style of decision-making used by leaders at that point. There is one other possible type of leader, what may be called a Synergist. The Synergist may be the theoretical ideal, able to synergize the different styles, able to adapt his or her own style to the needs at any particular time. Is any leader capable of this adaptation? Bill Gates of Microsoft has taken his company from its earliest entrepreneurial stage to a stage of significant maturity and complexity. Michael Dell appears to be similarly successful. May they at some point reach a condition of ease and become bureaucratic or aristocratic? Only history will tell.

Because an organization is a living system, much like the human body, it undergoes change even when seeming to standing still. Everyone has heard, "Why should we change? Nothing is broken. We are doing well." If you are doing nothing, you are standing still. From a systems viewpoint, standing still allows entropy or slow death to occur. The fact is that we all live in a global business environment that constantly imposes new challenges and requires adaptation. For example, some companies like airlines and utilities are in industries undergoing deregulation; therefore, change is imposed industry-wide. Others face rapidly evolving technology or increasingly sophisticated customers. It is not a question of whether to change or not.

The real questions are how dramatic the change needs to be and what style of leadership is required. Good leaders know when to exhibit the correct style and type of decision-making. They are aware of the organization and where it is in the life cycle. They are sensitive to internal and external conditions, trends, and pressures. Leaders must recognize the challenges faced by the organization and be able to choose the type of change required by those challenges.

The following categories represent typical levels of challenge and corresponding leadership responses. Try to identify the stage that most corresponds to your own organization.

Declining Culture: Cultures in decline are often led by those who are more concerned with their person, their power, their prestige, and perquisites than with common good, common vision, and noble purpose. The leader may be the Aristocrat who becomes alienated and aloof from his or her followers, or the Bureaucrat more concerned with order, compliance, and cost cutting than with conquering any new territory. The culture lacks a common focus, a clear sense of values or an awareness of threats from the environment. The culture is literally incapable of responding to challenges, not because of technical capability, but because of lack of creativity or energy. This is a loss of self-determination. The culture is committing suicide.

Holding Ground: Organizations that are dominated by a bureaucratic or administrative leadership style tend to be more concerned with maintaining their position rather than conquering new territory. They don't recognize any significant challenge to their position, and therefore see little reason to engage in significant change. Their response to financial pressures will be to cut costs rather than seek new sources of revenue or new market positions. Often, the perception of little challenge to the organization is a false sense of security, a failure to recognize challenges or to create new opportunities.

Gradually Improving: At this stage, the leaders are likely to be engineers or sales/marketing managers who are focused on the evolution of products and markets and are going about improvement in a systematic and orderly manner. They are likely to recognize challenges that will be in the development of competitor's products or new technologies. They may, however, miss challenges that are more revolutionary, such as the possible emergence of an entirely new application or new market. These leaders are likely to engage in gradual evolution of management practices, but without any revolutionary zeal

Rapidly Improving: Now the environment is presenting a more clear threat or opportunity, a significant challenge. The leader may still be the Builder or Explorer, but will have a bit of the Barbarian's determination to make change happen. The leader is often torn between his or her desire to maintain order in the system and the recognition that significant changes need to occur. This tension between order and change is a key theme in the organization, with some manager more focused on maintaining order and control and others pushing for more dramatic change. The leader needs to work to develop consensus strategies and plans with his senior team.

Strategic Challenge Matrix

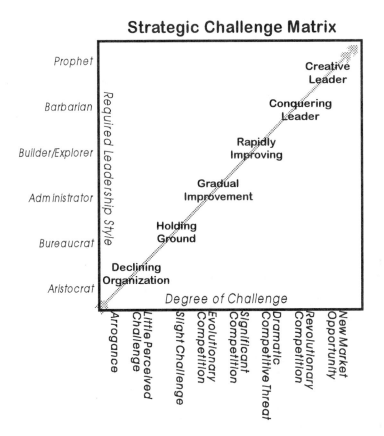

Conquering Leader: The leader is now the Barbarian whose motivation is dominated by a clear mission to conquer territory or create other dramatic change. The threat or opportunity from the environment is clear. The leader is in a fight for survival and will not accept minor adjustments to the system. Dramatic changes in organization, frequent changes in personnel, and a high level of stress are likely in this stage. Do not expect the ideal consensus decision-making environment. You can expect the leader to act much like a military commander. Although he or she may consult with others on decisions and gain input, there will be little time for drawn out decision processes.

Creative Leader: This stage is likely when a company is just formed and the entrepreneur is the inventor of the new product or service. This is a very high risk time for an organization because survival is very much in doubt. The leader will tend to gather around him a band of true believers who are likely to work exceeding long hours for the "cause," the new product, the new vision, the dream that motivates the creative leader. Any employee in this organization should have a high tolerance for ambiguity, chaotic change, unclear plans, and great risk. At the same time, this is the time of greatest opportunity.

There are times when the internal environment is incapable of responding to the external environment, and success is impossible. This point would be off the chart to the bottom left.

Chapter Eight

Team Management: The Core Practice of A High Performance Organization

The seamless organization, the learning organization, the reengineered, world-class, virtual, total quality organization. We are bombarded by terms that attempt to define the organization of the future. We know the goal. We want an organization that delights our customers, causes continuous improvement in products and services, minimizes cycle time, lowers costs and improves creativity and productivity. But what is the core practice, daily life, in such an organization? How does it affect the individual and cause the manager and employee to behave in a different way? How does the individual have to change? What are the principles and skills that guide individual behavior?

There are a few key characteristics of high performance organizations today. They can be summarized as follows:

- High acceptance of responsibility for business performance at every level.
- High information access and sharing.
- Regular and rigorous process measurement and analysis.
- High contact with customers and focus on their requirements.
- Flexibility and adaptability to changing markets and technology.
- High teamwork at every level of the organization.

Team management is a disciplined methodology, involving all employees in an organization, to create a high performance culture with each of these characteristics. Team management is, first and foremost, a system of managing performance through the total involvement of every employee working toward aligned, measurable, performance goals.

Team management is the practice of daily life in a high performance organization. Team management is a description of the new relationships between employees, their manager and their organization. Team management is the vehicle for every employee to become a true business manager with his or her personal goals aligned with the business goals of the organization.

We have been involved in the implementation of team practices for twenty years. In the early days this was as simple as the first line supervisor in a manufacturing plant getting his employees together once a week to review their performance and to "catch someone doing something good." This simple process of each supervisor placing charts and graphs of performance visibly on the wall, having weekly team discussions and recognition, produced significant and consistent improvements in productivity and quality. However, we soon realized it was difficult, if not impossible to keep this practice going at the first line if the supervisor was treated in a contrary way by his department manager. The department manager had to become a team leader. So to the plant manager with his department manager. The entire plant, division, and in many cases the entire company became a total team system with every employee participating in reviewing measurable business performance, setting goals, and experiencing the satisfaction of participating in improvement.

Eastman Chemicals, Delmarva Power and Light, Preston Trucking and others have maintained this team management practice for more than ten years and have experienced sustained high levels of quality and business performance. The natural work team structure is the core work practice at Honda, Toyota, Saturn and other world class companies.

As we have recognized the need for dramatic changes in organizational structure and systems we have been frequently reminded of the necessity to develop new skills and style, those of an effective team based organization, if the new architecture is to succeed.

While we began the team process twenty years ago at the first level of the organization, today we are finding that some of the most significant improvements derive from enhancing teamwork at the senior management levels. Unfortunately, the ability to function well as a team and to problem solve and reach unity on decisions is lacking among most senior management groups. The impact of unclear decisions, poorly developed and executed action plans, and disunity on decisions is felt throughout the organization. It is our view that the senior management team bears the burden of modeling that behavior, that culture, they wish to develop throughout their organization. If they wish to develop an organization that is able to make clear and effective decisions with rapid execution, they must develop their own team skills. If they wish the employees to be focused on performance and customers, they too must develop their own balanced scorecard with clear measures of business/financial performance as well as quality/process performance.

Structuring an organization into teams should be seen as a strategic initiative to achieve operational effectiveness. Strategic positioning is essential to long term performance. However, strategic position and focus, absent and effective organization will not lead to successful sustained performance. It is designed to improve the bottom line of the organization's performance. Teams are not an end in themselves but a means to involve people in managing their piece of the business more effectively.

Participating in a team is not voluntary any more than other management practices such as budgeting, appraising performance and tracking quality and productivity should be a choice. Working together on teams was voluntary when the teams were a form of quality circle that worked on a "problem," a very different process than the ongoing management of performance. Team management is not merely involvement, it is empowerment. Teams are assigned authority and responsibility for a specific process and for specific performance.

What is a *"high performance* team?"

1. A team with clear responsibility for business performance.
2. A team that knows its customers, suppliers and has a documented process known to all members.
3. A team with a balanced scorecard linked to organization performance.
4. A team with built in flexibility and adaptability through multi-skilled members who share functions.
5. A team that has demonstrated competence at problem solving by improving their work processes.

Teams should be empowered to make decisions concerning their portion of the business rather than merely making recommendations to higher levels of authority. While team structures may change and people will serve on several teams, teams should be seen as a permanent fixture in the organization, not a temporary answer to a business crisis or quality problem. It is worth considering that for most of humankind's life on this planet the natural work structure was the small group

- the family farm or craft shop. Large buildings and specialized, narrow, responsibilities with individuals working alone, is a recent phenomena of the mass production organization. Much of the disfunctions of the mass production organization are due to individual isolation and the absence of the "family" structure in the workplace. The team process renews what was natural for a million years - small groups of people sharing responsibility for shared work.

Understanding the Process

There are some basic steps in the team management process. While each team will respond to their own work process and priorities, at some point in the process each team should do the following:

1. Define Team Principles: All groups, whether families, athletic teams or work teams function well when they have common understanding priorities and principles. Define your team's principles around your organization's vision and how you want to work as a team. Principles may include things such as the agreement to conduct discussions with absolute frankness and honesty; to agree to adhere to decision in unity as if they were your own; to listen to all input with respect; and to maintain a constant focus on the requirements of customers.

2. Clarify Roles and Responsibilities: One of the most common misunderstandings of team management is that teams reduce responsibility and result in the chaos unclear roles. If one had never seen a basketball game and walked into the arena it might appear to be chaos with players running every which way in apparent disorder. However, the more one understands the sport, the more one understands that there are very clear roles and responsibilities, designed plays and discipline. The same is true with management and work teams. Roles may include facilitation, data collection and presentation, customer and supplier communication, training, and responsibility for specific process steps.

3. Define Key Customers and Requirements: Reports that "quality is dead" are premature. Without a doubt one of the most useful concepts to come out of the quality movement is the focus on customers and their requirements. The team management process institutionalizes this focus as a routine responsibility of every employee on every team. Each team will decide how best to define their customers and how to gather data on requirements. They may interview their customers, gather survey or telephone information, and will seek to develop ongoing customer feedback on their performance. They will also define their suppliers and share their requirements with their suppliers.

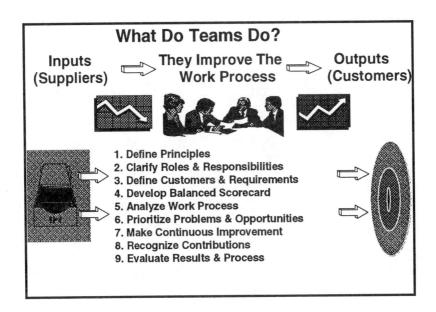

4. Develop a Balanced Scorecard: The purpose of the team management process is to improve business performance. Each and every team should know their data. They should define measures that reflect the output of their work process as well as measures of customer satisfaction. Measures typically include productivity, quality, costs and cycle time. It is generally the practice to develop a visual scoreboard so that every team member can see the graphs moving toward their goal and experience the emotional impact of improved (or the reverse!) performance. Scorecards are generally reviewed at each team meeting and form the basis for ongoing problem solving and performance improvement efforts.

5. Analyze the Work Processes: Teams are formed around responsibility for specific work processes. The processes may be assembling a certain product in a manufacturing environment, servicing a group of customers, selling to a defined market group, or for a senior management team, developing business strategy. Each team should be expert in those processes for which it is responsible. To be expert in a work process that process must be defined, its course mapped, its cycle time measured and alternatives considered. A requirement of ISO 9000 is that definition and management of processes. This is also a requirement of the team process. It is from this analysis and knowledge that is formed the basis for continuous improvement.

6. Prioritize Problems: Problems are a normal part of all work environments. It is the purpose of teams to assume ownership of all problems related to their work process and to solve those problems in the most effective and rapid manner. Teams are trained in data analysis and problem solving techniques.

7. Recognize Contributions: In past years managers were encouraged to "catch-someone-doing-something-good-today" on the assumption that it was they who were responsible for the performance of their people. While that is still true, it is also true in a high performing organization that all employees share in the responsibility to celebrate success, to recognize the accomplishments of their peers and teams. Many teams include recognition as a regular item on their meeting agendas. One results of the team process is to make the work place a more satisfying place of employment.

8. Evaluate: Evaluation of the entire process, from customer requirements, to work process, to results, to the functioning of the group as a team is an ongoing responsibility of the team. By periodic evaluation the team develops the sensitivity and flexibility to make adjustments as they develop greater skill and as circumstances change.

Leadership's Role

In creating a team-based organization, there are some critical change agents. These change agents all have a role in the success of the process. They are the leadership team who steer the process; the team consultants or coaches who assist the teams in their assimilation of the new skills; and the customers and suppliers to the organization and to the teams.

The leadership team has the following role:

1. Define the mission, vision, and values: What is our purpose as an organization? Who do we want to become in relation to our market place? The vision includes the questions, "What it will be like to work here?" and, "What performance results do we expect to be achieving?" These outcomes should be the focus of the change effort. Every decision they then make should be evaluated under the lens of this future vision. The core values will guide conduct of the teams and individuals. The team process can be the vehicle to make these active through the organization.

2. Plan the change process. The senior team should be heavily involved in planning the improvement effort with their change agents. If the senior team does not understand all the implications of the change effort, it often leaves the consultants or coaches without the credibility to move the process forward.

3. Learn and practice. The senior team should undergo all the same training and implementation steps expected of the rest of the organization. It is our experience that teamwork at the top is often no better than below and more critical in arriving at effective and unifying decisions. This enables them both to practice their skills within their own team as well as to "testify" to the impact it has had on them personally.

4. Model the desired behavior. One of the keys to effective leadership is to become the model of the desired behavior. Every individual in the organization will be watching the senior team to see if their behavior changes during the implementation process. Questions will always surface such as, "Do they make team decisions? What does their scorecard look like?"

5. Reinforce improvement. The only way organizations survive the agonies of rearranging themselves is through experiencing success along the way. The senior team needs to play an active role in giving recognition to those who are even attempting to change. It's a mistake to wait for the "big hits."

6. Evaluate results. Just as in the Shewhart cycle of Plan-Do-Check-Act, the senior team needs to constantly evaluate the results of their efforts to plan the next move. This cycle is the spirit of continuous improvement. Don't look for a "finish line"; think of this cycle as a life-style change to make the organization continuously healthier and more competitive.

Change Agent's Role

The development of new skills requires more than knowledge. It requires training, practice and immediate feedback. This is the role of the coaches or consultants. They will also help with practical problem solving and application. They need to be well respected by the organization, effective communicators, passionate about the change effort, and competent in the techniques of team decision making. They can make the following contributions to the process.

1. Advise on the development of a project plan.

2. Train and provide feedback to their team leaders and members.

3. "Contract" with each team leader and team regarding the steps in the development of the team and steps toward performance improvement.

4. Diagnose their process and helping teams solve particular implementation problems. The change agents often help facilitate solutions between teams or with systemic problems within the organization.

5. Reinforce positive behavior change. Until managers develop the habit of reinforcing their subordinates for their successful practices, this is an important role for change agents.

6. Evaluation is a constant process to determine appropriate next steps towards continuous improvement.

Customers and Suppliers

Customers and suppliers affect all the inputs and outputs of the team. They either control what comes into the team (suppliers) or accept or reject what the team produces (customers). Obviously a close relationship with both stakeholders is critical to the team's success. This is just as true whether the team is on the factory floor, in the public relations, engineering or human resource department. Customers and suppliers make the following contributions to the team management process.

1. Have a clearly defined relationship with the team. Some even choose to participate in the team's meetings on a regular basis.

2. Clearly define the customer requirements of the team's output.

3. Provide input to the team's work process.

4. Provide feedback to the team.

5. Participate in evaluating the results of the team's improvement efforts.

Team Management Results

Team management is a system of management. It is not a program. It is an investment in the performance of the organization. It must produce results or it is a bad investment. The team management process has consistently demonstrated business results and, therefore, has become a lasting practice in our client organizations. The following are a few examples:

1. The two most admired oil companies, according to *Fortune Magazine*, are Shell and Amoco. We helped both implement the team process extensively and it has become the ongoing management process from top to bottom in their domestic exploration/production organizations. They have reported financial results in the hundreds of millions of dollars.

2. Delmarva Power and Light, beginning twelve years ago, began implementing the team process beginning with the Chairman's own team. That process led to Delmarva becoming the power company with the highest customer satisfaction ratings and the best quality performance in the industry. They never pursued the recognition of quality prizes, just of their customers.

3. Tennesse Eastman, now Eastman Chemicals, began implementing the team process with our help ten years ago. This process has been maintained and became the foundation for many other practices which led their winning the Malcom Baldrige Award.

4. The McDonald's Corporation, in somewhat of a controlled experiment, implemented our team process in specific areas of the country. These areas have experienced significantly higher rates of performance improvement than other areas. The practice is now being expanded.

These are a few specific cases that we have assisted. In general, you can expect the following results from the team management process.

Motivation and a Sense of Belonging

Why do we enjoy playing on teams? Teams celebrate success together, suffer their losses together, and form bonds of friendship around the activity of the team. Teams have fun because they have common goals, keep score, and gain the satisfaction of succeeding together. It is natural for teams to try to perform to the best of their ability. Teams also become important social groups that provide a sense of belonging and recognition of individual contributions which enhance self-esteem.

Improved Communication

The team process involves everyone in the organization. Both employees and managers serve on teams. Teams are forums for communication. Communication is more efficient because the group discusses, asks questions, and clarifies decisions together. A question that is on the minds of many is often asked by one person. Efficiency and morale are improved when members of a team have the same information and feel that information is being shared freely.

Lasting Behavior Change

Many training programs produce a temporary boost in performance. People get excited and behave differently for a short while; then things often return to the old, routine way. This happens because a new, better system of management that involves everyone has not been created. Team management creates systems that lead to permanent changes. .

Shared Learning From a Diverse Workforce

Teams provide the employee with an opportunity to contribute particular strengths to the larger group and to learn from the strengths of others. Each of us is "wired" differently. We think differently, analyze the world differently, and present our thoughts and ideas in various ways. Teams are a vehicle for capturing the richness afforded us through our diversity. Individuals also learn to value the different competencies and ideas of others within the team.

Performance Results

In the team management process, every employee becomes a business manager. One of the most powerful components of the team process is the development of a balanced scorecard by every team. This scorecard includes business and customer satisfaction measures; or financial and process measures. This scorecard is generally posted and visible to each team member each day. It is the focus of discussion and action planning. It is normal for teams to demonstrate improvements in costs, quality, productivity, and cycle time.

When we began the development of the team process nearly twenty years ago in small textile mills in the Carolinas we had no idea that similar processes would be proven to be the core of the Toyota Production System and be adopted as increasingly common practice among the world's most admired companies. The development of high performance teams and team-based organizations is here to stay. The only issue now is how best to structure the process and manage the change. This is the focus of our efforts.

Chapter Nine

Corporate Center Strategy

The two critical issues of achieving successful business performance, strategic positioning and operational effectiveness, most often lead to improvement efforts in the operating units of a company. However, the performance of the corporate center, its ability to add unique value, and its costs, are also important consideration for leaders of significant performance improvement.

In a highly cost competitive environment the role of the corporate center has been an increasing focus. The issue is confounded by the variety of roles of corporate centers in different companies. Successful companies like Merck, 3M, and Intel have strong corporate centers with centralized functions such as research and development, human resource management, manufacturing, engineering, and management, and information technology. There are other successful companies such as ABB that have a large divisional structure, but only a handful of managers at the corporate center.

Absent a clear purpose, a focus on strategic contribution to value, the corporate (or division) center can be a primary source of inefficiency. Corporate staffs, like central governments, even though comprised of the most competent and best intentioned individuals, can create project after project, report after report, review after review. Each activity is intended to create some value, but together they often deplete the energies and divert the focus of those who serve customers and create revenue. If the business units, plants, or other operations are to be redesigned for effectiveness, so too must the corporate center be redesigned to focus on creating value and efficiency.

This chapter is intended to help the executive team define the value-added function of the corporate center.

What is the role of the corporation, or headquarters, as distinct from the operating divisions? Do the corporate headquarters, executives, staffs, and budgets add value, or do they merely impose an additional cost burden on the revenue generating business units? This is a question being asked by many corporations. The answer has profound implications for the structure of the organization, its work processes, the human competencies, the size and budget of headquarters, and the relationships and processes that flow across business units.

Strategic Options

Each of the following options may be appropriate for different corporations at different times. An understanding of these options largely defines the role of corporate executives and staffs. Your task as a corporate strategist is first to decide which of these core strategies are relevant to your firm and then decide the substantive direction, or how these strategies will be executed. With each of these strategies there are associated work processes and human competencies. After identifying which of these is the primary strategy for adding corporate value in your firm, you then define measures of strategic success; the appropriate work processes; the competencies associated with the strategy; and the structure to provide for development and accountability.

If none of these options are appropriate to a corporation it is likely that the corporation is depleting rather than adding value, and this is likely to be reflected in the stock price. An example of this was the General Motors structure in which it was estimated that if the Automotive, Hughes Electronics, EDS and parts groups were split off they would be valued by the market at about 150-200% of current market value. Each of the separate businesses is capable of employing the strategies of integration and scale independently. There are no economies of scale and integration across Hughes, EDS, and automotive, for example. Corporate functions only add additional cost burden to their performance.

An additional layer of management above that which adds value is most likely to reduce responsiveness and increase cost. One theory of strategic success, promoted recently by Alfred Chandler, is the theory of challenge and response. It is not so much which strategy a firm selects that leads to success as it is the ability of management to identify challenges from the environment and from within and respond vigorously and appropriately. The extra weight of additional layers of management reduces this ability.

1. Economies of Integration: Through sharing resources, such as human resources, information, capital, or technology, the capability of each division is enhanced. Procter and Gamble or other consumer marketing companies have economies of integration through shared market research, marketing resources, and distribution channels. Different consumer product divisions have access to capabilities they could not afford on their own. This integration may reduce costs but it may also provide market access or market intelligence that would be unavailable to non-integrated divisions.

2. Economies of Scale: By combining divisions under a corporate umbrella and the mere increase in volume, there may be lower costs. These costs include purchasing supplies, research, and marketing. This is the Sears or General Motors advantage. General Motors can leverage research in engine technology, safety, and fuel economy across more cars sold, thus reducing the cost per unit of that research. They can also purchase in quantities that may result in lower costs. Large retail organizations have a similar advantage. Those functions that create these economies, engineering or purchasing, for example, logically are corporate center functions.

3. Economies of Allocation: This advantage is one of capital formation and capital flow. With multiple divisions competing for capital and contributing capital to a common pool, the corporate managers can allocate capital resources to those divisions that can predict the highest returns. This was the assumption of ITT and many other conglomerates for many years. This was the assumption of "portfolio strategy" that was dominant during the 1960's and 1970's. Allocation strategy is likely to be incompatible with integration strategy. Allocation strategy assumes competition; integration strategy assumes cooperation and sharing. A clear choice between these strategies is desirable rather than attempting to blend them.

4. Managerial Competence: One explanation for competitive success is competence. Competence may be either technical or managerial. Technical competence may be sufficiently concentrated in a business unit. However, managerial competence may be better developed across divisions so managers have an opportunity to share experience, tools, models, and people. General Electric is considered by many to be the most managerially competent corporation in America. Whether true or not, GE has worked very hard at developing, sharing, and leveraging managerial competence.

5. Brand Equity: Value is created by current cash flow and by the ability to create future cash flow. The ability to create future cash flow due to positive consumer perception of a brand name is brand equity. Sara Lee's primary corporate strategy is based on building and capitalizing on brand equity through brands such as L'Eggs, Champion, Hanes, etc. Coca-Cola may be the most widely recognized brand in the world. Coke is the champion of shareholder value largely because of its competence at building and exploiting the Coke brand and leveraging this to brands such as Sprite, Minute Maid, Fruitopia, and others. This brand management is the core competence and core process at Coca-Cola headquarters.

Firm Characteristics by Strategy

It may be helpful to consider the nature of firms that find each of the five possible headquarters strategies appropriate and how these strategies affect their internal functioning.

1. Economies of Integration

The Challenge & Environment: There are two forms of integration: process and competence. Firms that employ process integration as a successful strategy have business units whose business creates highly dependent relationships with other businesses. The automotive business is an example in the integration of automotive production and financing. Clearly, the automotive dealer must be able to finance, and the ease of financing will impact car sales. It would present an obvious disadvantage if the dealer had no financing arm. The ease of financing, and the opportunity to profit from this service, represents an obvious economy of integration. Similar process integration exists in oil exploration, production, refining, and marketing.

Integration of competence is found in technology companies such as TRW, Hughes, Intel, or Mitsubishi. While there are different business units serving different markets (automotive, aerospace, and telecommunications in the case of TRW and Hughes) there are common engineering skills and patented devices (semi-conductors for example) that can be deployed across business units. Hughes is employing its satellite technology in DirectTV, military applications, and commercial telecommunications. These companies have the ability to enter a new market and create a new business unit because of their competence in the technology. Therefore, the management of this technology is a core capability of the corporate center.

Structure & Incentives: The structure of these firms will include strong business unit structures with headquarters functions that assure shared information of mutual advantage between units. This might include market and price prediction and premise planning (such as Shell scenario planning), information integration to facilitate flow through the units, and shared management development and human resources to create a common culture and knowledge among executives across business units. There is not likely to be strong central financial control or competition for capital, but rather a P&L accountability and incentive. Those that have integrating competencies are likely to have central core research and development organizations and may have processes in place to share learning and technological developments across the business units.

2. Economies of Scale

Challenge & Environment: Large manufacturing organizations have long been among those who organized around the principle of economies of scale. These firms include a high material input or content into their production process and therefore large purchasing dollars. Airlines, although a service business, are also examples of economies of scale. In order to maintain equipment and repair bases, a scale of utilization is required. Purchasing airplanes and fuel also present the economic advantages that make large-scale purchasing an advantage. These firms are also likely to have numerous and similar operations that can be compared in performance. Textile companies or aluminum can manufacturers have numerous similar plants. This creates the opportunity for comparing and controlling performance among these plants, as well as controlling production input by leveling production among plants.

Structure and Incentives: These firms are likely to have strong central purchasing and selling organizations that may be leveraged across the operations. This tends to reduce authority in each operation. This authority may be further reduced by the ability to manage and control input flow and compare performance. Because of the similarity of process there are also likely to be strong central engineering organizations. These firms will often have staff groups, both production and accounting, that are in the business of monitoring and evaluating performance. It is these elements that have caused many of these firms to take on relatively autocratic management practices and create strong and adversarial headquarters operations. The examples of Honda and Toyota demonstrate that more participative styles are possible, although these firms have also led the movement toward lean production (Toyota Production System) which deals with the economies of scale in new ways. These new ways assume very tight coordination between customers and suppliers at the first level and a degree of competence and communication through the supply chain not common in most economy of scale organizations.

3. Economies of Allocation

Challenge & Environment: These firms emerged from corporations with low rates of innovation and internal business expansion and with slow growth but highly profitable operations. This allowed the redeployment of capital to the purchase of new and non-integrated businesses. All of these firms face the challenge of managing businesses without similar core competencies across business units. ITT in the United States and Hanson Trust in the UK became typical of this type of firm.

Structure and Incentives: The primary process and competence of the headquarters operation in these firms is financial control and management. Ideally these firms engage in strategic review of return and growth, allowing the business unit managers to focus on operational management. However, because of the perceived financial expertise of headquarters, there is a strong tendency to review short-term operational financial management. This is dangerous absent operational expertise, knowledge of markets, and operational processes. This tendency has led many of these firms to be viewed as over-controlling and autocratic. It may also lead to a failure to appreciate the value of operational competence over financial competence and produce business failure, as was the case in many ITT business units. In the headquarters of these firms there should be little in the way of human resource management, marketing, engineering, information technology (other than financial), research and development, or management development. This is the headquarters that can manage a large number of business units with a staff of twenty due to the absence of integration.

4. Managerial Competence

Challenge and Environment: The pursuit of managerial competence is usually a strategy in addition to one of the above strategies. Every firm would like to have superior management ability. This does not qualify as a strategy unless the firm is acting to capture this advantage in very deliberate ways, and most firms are not. This firm may operate in an environment that does not provide for many other advantages other than superior execution and delivery to the market. GE headquarters does not provide research and development or other integrating advantages across plastics, aircraft engines, and financial services. GE could become a headquarters based largely on allocation strategy unless it focused its energies on managerial competence and performance. It may be this focus that has distinguished GE from firms such as ITT that failed to create a focus on non-financial management processes and competence. Many superior performing companies that have clear integration strategies, such as Intel, have succeeded largely because of superior execution due to superior managerial competence.

Structure and Incentives: These firms' headquarters are likely to have strong financial management and review processes that create high accountability for performance, coupled with strong central human resource and management development processes. They are likely to lack strong central research and development.

5. Brand Equity

Challenge and Environment: Firms that focus on the creation of brand equity are likely to operate in a consumer marketing environment and have strong brand identity. They may be built upon their initial brand equity with the fortunate success of one brand and then face the challenge of leveraging that asset to the creation of additional brands to penetrate additional market segments. Reliance on one brand is a dangerous strategy given the rapid changes in consumer preference in certain markets. The challenge to duplicate the initial brand asset is the primary challenge while continued marketing for position, recognition, and market share are the ongoing focus.

Structure and Incentives: These firms will often have a strong supply/manufacturing side of the business to serve the dominant consumer marketing/brand management side. Both of these functions will be centralized at headquarters. They are also likely to have strong centralized research and development, financial management, legal, and human resource organizations. Incentives are clearly focused on market share, market growth, and new brand launches.

By defining which of these five strategies is most appropriate, the senior management team can provide a basis for analyzing the value of each corporate process, staff and expense. The strategy creates a standard. If the core strategy of the corporate center is managerial excellence it will be worth evaluating the staffing and funding of these activities in relationship to financial staffing associated with capital allocation strategy. Once the executives have determined the appropriateness of the strategies the design team should assess the capabilities, the organization structure, and the process performance that supports the strategy. This is

Chapter Ten

Finally - At Least Do This!

Ok, we know you're not going to do everything recommended in this book. But, if you are at all serious about creating change in your organization, for heaven's sake at least do the following few, critical things.

Own the Charter: Make It Significant!

The Whole System Architecture process described in this book and the *Change Management workbook* is designed to create "significant" change, an improved strategic position, not continuous improvement which generally involves many small steps. The ongoing Team Management process is focused on continuous improvement in operational effectiveness. The design charter is the basic document that sets direction, the agenda, the priorities and the boundaries for the design team. It is your responsibility to assure that the design team receives guidance and the challenge that will make their work meaningful and significant.

The charter could be described as having two components: one is the more general principles, the future organization's "golden rules." One person has described these elements as "vanilla," all sounding the same. They do sound much the same because they largely repeat the principles stated in the corporate mission, vision or values statements. While similar, they are still important, just as "freedom of speech" is important in our constitution, although it may appear in more than one document.

The second component of the charter is specific to your business and process. This is includes the definition of specific capabilities, technical and human, required to achieve an improved market position. It also includes specific performance targets for business units and enabling processes. It includes a focus on which core processes are most important to strategic success. Defining these components of the charter are essential responsibilities of the leaders of the organization. This is the strategy for your organization and should not be taken lightly.

There is little that an executive does more important than setting the strategy for his or her organization. All strategy may be divided into two types: external (market and financial) strategy; and internal (organizational capabilities). Internal strategy requires an analysis of the current capabilities, technical and human, the forces that will drive change, and a definition of the future market and required capabilities.

The senior team of an organization needs to take the time to consult together, to think together, to imagine the future together, to apply their higher intellectual abilities to the future of the business and organization and reach a shared consensus view of the future. This common understanding can only result from a process that involves shared thinking and that requires time. Unfortunately, most executives choose not to make this time. They will say that they "don't have the time." We tend to find time for issues that are urgent, and don't have time for things that are important. What could be more important than defining the future work of the organization and creating the capabilities to perform that work? It may, however, not be as urgent as the third revision of the budget due next week.

It is also important that the charter contain significant performance objectives. What do you expect to accomplish with this design process? With several clients we have had goals to cut cycle time by 50%, increase output per employee, reduce defects by 50%, etc. It is desirable, although not absolutely necessary, to provide the design teams with these types of goals.

This Is *Business* Architecture

While the new architecture should try to create a more desirable future organization and culture it is important to understand this process as business driven. The emphasis on process, culture and business drivers needs to be decided by the senior steering team. However, keep in mind that it is easy to experience process "drift" unless the business drivers are clearly defined.

One way to establish this focus is to have the steering team act as *The Investor* who will allocate future business resources based on the analysis conducted during the development of the new architecture. The steering team might decide that every organizational unit will have 30% less capital in two years, 50% less capital in four years, as a base-case assumption. The design teams, into justify the capital expense of their organization above this level will have to present a business case for the expenditure of that capital. Would it be a good investment decision to manufacture a component in-house or reduce that capital requirement and outsource the manufacturing? Can we justify current research expenditures based on a financial analysis of potential return and what is it about the new organizational design that will make this investment more attractive than previous such investments or alternatives?

Starting with a base assumption of drastic reductions and having to consider the business case for additional expenditures will dramatically focus the thinking of the design team. The steering team should make clear that this is not a "game" they are playing, but that this is input into real decision making concerning future resource allocation. This investment-analysis view of the design process is valuable because many of the members of both steering teams and design teams are not in the habit of viewing the organization as a set of assets that are required to produce competitive rates of return. This process can be applied to enabling processes such as information technology, human resources, and engineering support, as well as the core processes.

Communicate, Communicate, Communicate

Many executives have emerged from disciplines that required the development of linear thinking: engineering, accounting, the sciences. They believe in the straight line with fixed beginning and end points.

To communicate why we are redesigning the organization they will send out a message, often in writing, stating very clearly the intent and method of redesign. Done! They have done this job. They check it off. One month later they are surprised and frustrated to find that employees didn't get the message, have dozens of strange interpretations, many being the worst of all possible interpretations.

In my experience, marketing based organizations do a far better job of communicating than engineering or production companies. Marketing driven companies have executives with far better understanding of communications. They understand image. They understand that people remember what they feel. They understand that messages must be repeated over and over in order to build trust in the message. They understand that the first time a message is communicated only ten percent of the recipients understand it, fifty percent have confused understanding and forty percent didn't get it at all! This is normal.

We suggest you plan communication of the desired change to include...

- Repeated live presentations by key executives

- Newsletters describing examples of the desired type of organization

- Videos with examples and discussions by executives

- Communicating specific changes that executives are making in their personal style and behavior

- Share the charter

- Periodic communication of the progress of the design teams

- Tune your radar screen to find examples of desired behavior and highlight these examples as positive models in your own organization

- Develop symbols of the new organization

- Personal stories work best. Develop your own personal stories illustrating the change

Reinforce the Design Teams:

The design teams will require anywhere from four to eight months to complete their analysis and redesign. During this time they will be working hard, but more important, they will be struggling with significant decisions. For example, many design team members have designed their own jobs out of the organization. They have designed superiors and subordinates jobs away. They have eliminated symbols to which they have become attached. They have made decisions that they expected would draw fire from peers as well as superiors. If they make significant decisions, they will make difficult decisions.

They need to know that you are behind them, that you genuinely support their efforts, even thought you may not accept every recommendation. They need to know that they are working with you, for you, not against you.

You can accomplish this support by meeting with the design team periodically. Drop in on them unexpectedly and ask them how they are doing. Have lunch with them. And, tell the that you are expecting breakthroughs, "out-of-village" thinking, that will lead to genuine advantages. They will need to hear this more than once.

Seamless at the Top:

A seamless organization is an organization with continuous process flow, no interruptions, or redo loops. If functions as one organism with a common pulse or heart-beat. It will be absolutely impossible to create a seamless organization at lower levels if the senior executives are not seamless in their own process and behavior. Most senior executive groups are not viewed as seamless today.

The senior executives, division heads, of Motorola are required by the Chairman to spend 30% of their time working together on corporate strategic issues, forcing them to delegate management functions to subordinates. The senior executives of Shell Oil, Amoco, Tennessee Eastman, Honda and others have regular team meetings in which they address common goals, problems, and help each other problem solve. They develop common views, consensus decisions, and can then represent the interests of the corporation, not just their silo, to their subordinates.

High performing organizations are team based because teams are the basic unit in which people work together as one. It is in teams that individuals contribute to the larger whole, whether on the factory floor or the boardroom. Great teams have players that will sacrifice for one another, give up the ball, hand off, run plays as if one. This is seamless.

It is a widely reported perception that senior executives in some companies meet together, but do not always share their true views or feelings; agree to decisions, but then leave and tell others why the decision was wrong; listen politely to others in the meeting, then leave and tell subordinates about the mistaken views or statements to which they listened without comment. Senior executives at these companies do not demonstrate the skills of effective group decision making or problem solving. This greatly reinforces "silo" behavior.

When executives begin a reengineering effort they are thinking about the cost savings, the improved cycle times and reduction of bureaucracy. They often do not associate this with their own behavior. But, their own behavior is linked, and in some measure the cause and solution.

Two years ago we began working with a senior team of a large international company. When we interviewed the senior executives we asked them questions about how decisions were made and it quickly became apparent that there was no "senior team." The senior executive met with the VP of finance when dealing with financial issues. He then called in the human resource manager to make decisions about compensation or staffing. He then met with the VP of operations to get updates on production, safety and costs. The never met together. And it should be no surprise that the operating managers felt that the human resource manager was out of touch with the real needs of operations. The finance manager felt that the operating manager didn't appreciate the financial targets and strategy, etc.

For the first year we structured this group as a team, defined the decisions for which they shared responsibility, their common customers, common processes and worked to improve those processes together. They were trained to facilitate meetings, to brainstorm together, to reach consensus, to develop a team scorecard, to manage their meetings efficiently and prioritize their time. We sat in the majority of their meetings for the first year and coached the team and the leader.

At the beginning of the second year the structure was reconsidered. A layer of management was removed and all of the business unit operating managers (five) were added to the team. When We last observed this team the agenda was prepared by one of the business unit managers. Another member of the team facilitated the meeting. Another served as timekeeper. Another served a scribe to record decisions, action items and future agenda items. At the end of the meeting a volunteer was invited to facilitate the next meeting. The decisions were reviewed. An action item list was handed out. Finally, the meeting was evaluated by the group.

During this entire meeting, the Executive Vice President, who previously was considered to be highly autocratic and a poor listener, participated in a manner virtually indistinguishable from the other members. It was a true team meeting. It was a meeting in which frankness, sharing and learning, were visible. The team has defined their common customers, their balanced scorecard and defined their decision making process. Perhaps the most surprising view of this process is that the leader now feels that he has better control of his management group and tighter focus on performance. This is the team process at the top.

To change pattern of behavior will require a commitment on your part to learn and practice new skills. You will be asking all of your subordinates to do the same. They will only develop both the skills and spirit of teamwork if they see you learning and demonstrating these skills.

If the executives are willing to do these things the success of the change effort is virtually assured.

Appendix

A Brief History of Change

We fail the test of corporate memory. We run off in the direction of an exciting new solution, forgetting the lessons of previous teaching and experience, only to be pulled back in the disillusionment of relearning old lessons. We have a long history that pulls us magnetically toward a single prophet of future profits. Each year or two it appears that the world of management is running off on a new crusade in search of salvation.

If you have survived the management fads of the past twenty years it might be helpful to understand how this apparent disconnected chaos was a path, although twisted at times, leading us from a period of family business, farms or craft shops, to specialization of large scale production, and now back to a system again based on a family like structures of shared ownership and responsibility.

All management practice is an evolution of earlier practice. That which is considered excellent in management today is conditioned by footprints of earlier ideas. Methods of change are conditioned by the many efforts of those who have struggled on the path before.

There are seven major fields of knowledge and experience synthesized in whole system management. This is, simply, my learning history, the root structure of knowledge and experience upon which whole system management is founded. My[1] own learning history, to a large extent, parallels the learning and development of organization effectiveness and improvement practices. It is not necessary to know history to do the right things today. However, a generation of Americans growing up without an appreciation of the qualities, sentiments and experience of our Founding Fathers, for example, is a frightening prospect. Without collective memory a people are doomed to repeat the mistakes of the past

---

[1] This chapter represents the personal journey of the first author, hence the use of the personal pronoun.

and fail to appreciate their present condition. Without an appreciation of these sources of management experience you are likely to repeat the mistakes of history.

The first of these seven fields of knowledge is *behavioral or experimental psychology*. The second is *social and group psychology*. The third set involves the teachings of Dr. Deming, Juran, and others on the application of *quality management*. The fourth is *socio-technical systems design* and open systems theory. The fifth deals with the development, primarily in Japan, of *lean production* methods best seen in the Toyota Production System. The sixth is *business process reengineering*. The seventh is complexity theory which is similar to chaos theory. Whole system management is a unifying theory and process that incorporates the lessons of all these contributions.

Behavioral Psychology

I began my career in 1969 at Polk Youth Center, Department of Corrections, Raleigh, North Carolina. I was supposed to counsel, and I assumed reform, 350 young felons. I was to listen and talk my inmates into better attitudes and behavior. I soon realized the futility of this task. The power of the collective environment, the influence of other inmates, and the institutional system overwhelmed any positive influence. The problem was far greater than talk and ideas; it was the reality of the system. The individual could not be changed without dramatically altering the prison environment.

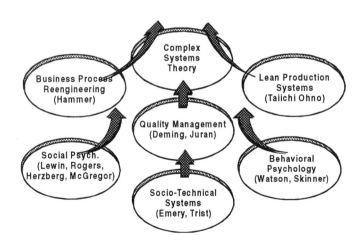

I soon learned the principles of behavior modification, the application in the natural environment of experimental psychology, the scientific exploration of Dr. B. F. Skinner and his followers. Dr. Deming says that managers must "know the facts," look at the data. If one has any respect for the scientific method, for statistics and true knowledge versus superstition, one cannot ignore the vast body of scientific research on the analysis of behavior.

My first major change effort was a government grant to redesign a medium security prison in North Carolina. I established a free economy in which all inmates were paid with a weekly check based on how well they performed in their work (it was in "points," not "real" money), and they paid rent for either a "luxury," "quality," "standard," or "efficiency" dorm. They also had to pay for movies and anything else considered desirable. Production in the work area doubled; negative behavior was dramatically reduced; learning in the school increased; and even verbal interaction between guards and inmates became more positive. A change in the system, in the architecture of the organization that delivered reinforcing consequences, produced dramatic changes in behavior.

A reengineered process, employee empowerment, and total quality management require a set of habit patterns. Old habits must be modified. Thanks to the work of Dr. Skinner[2] and his associates we know a great deal about how to change habits, how to construct the environment, how to deal with the contingencies of reinforcement, and how to optimize the probability of continuous improvement. [3] This is rarely incorporated in most current change processes.

Social Psychology

The field of organization development (OD) emerged primarily from the work of social psychologists, which took a very different focus than experimental psychology. Social psychology focused on human needs, feelings, and the dynamics between people in groups. Researchers and writers such as Kurt Lewin and Carl Rogers developed models to describe the interaction within groups and the patterns of communication between individuals.

---

[2] Skinner, B. F. *Science and Human Behavior*, New York, Free Press, 1953; and, *Contingencies of Reinforcement: A Theoretical Analysis*, New York, Appleton-Century-Crofts, 1969.

[3] Stolovitch, Harold D. and Keeps, Erica J. *Handbook of Human Performance Technology*, San Francisco, Jossey-Bass, 1992.

In 1954 Maslow defined seven stages of human motivation or needs. This structure was useful in helping managers understand the significance of motivational influences beyond the simple need for survival and money. Maslow's work and the work of Herzberg[4] and McGregor[5] further developed the understanding of the relationship between organizational systems, management styles (Theory X and Theory Y), and employee motivation. This work became the foundation upon which numerous management and organization development practices were built. Job enrichment[6], Blake and Mouton's Managerial Grid, and various forms of group training and team building all have their foundation in the principles and values promoted by social and humanistic psychology.

The development of Quality Circles in Japan can be traced back to the research in group dynamics and decision-making conducted in the 1950s in the United States. Somewhat strangely, group problem solving and team development have returned to this country through efforts to emulate Japanese problem solving and decision-making.

Total Quality Management

During the late seventies our work in industry (increasingly in service organizations) included forming employees into teams. We developed a *team management* process in which all managers were the leaders of their team and served on their superior's team. All team members plotted their data, set objectives, and solved problems. At the same time, the quality circle movement was becoming popular, and awareness of the importance of quality was just beginning.

During our earliest work the emphasis was on improving productivity and reducing absenteeism and turnover. With the growing popularity of quality management, we learned from Dr. Deming, Dr. Juran, and Phil Crosby to place the emphasis on performance to customer requirements, to define performance in terms of customer satisfaction, and

---

[4] Herzberg, Frederick. *Work and the Nature of Man*. World Publishing Company, 1966.

[5] McGregor, Douglas M. *The Human Side of Enterprise*. New York: McGaw-Hillk Book Company, Inc. 1960.

[6] Meyer, M. Scott. *Every Employee A Manager*. New York: McGraw-Hill Book Company. 1970.

to provide feedback to suppliers.[7] These views complemented our team management process. From Dr. Deming and his disciples we learned the importance of variability in process and of gaining statistical knowledge and control of the process. We increasingly had teams focus on the nature of their process. We also adopted fishbone diagrams, pareto analysis, and other problem-solving techniques from the toolbag of quality management.

Quality management reinforced our view of the importance of data, scientific knowledge, and the importance of systems. Dr. Deming repeatedly emphasized the power of the system and the importance of managing the system. I understood this from my experience in prisons and from reading Dr. Skinner's definition of a system of behavior analysis. Through our work with dozens of companies implementing a total team system from top to bottom, we had become convinced of the importance of changing the whole rather than separate parts of the organization which could easily drift back to their prior state. Unfortunately, Dr. Deming and the quality advocates provided no method for analyzing and changing the system.

Socio-Technical Systems (STS) Design

The fourth major contribution to our work came in the early eighties through my acquaintance with Norman Bodek of Productivity, Inc., who has done much to spread the knowledge of improvement methods. I became aware of socio-technical design and the work of Lou Davis, Dick Walton, Jack Sherwood, and William Pasmore.[8]

At this point work included most functions in the organization: manufacturing, sales, engineering, and staff groups. The simple emphasis on feedback and positive reinforcement had expanded to include the total team system and the necessary group problem-solving skills. We were increasingly bumping into structural and systems alignment problems. The old appraisal system did not take into account the new skills

---

[7] Deming, W. Edwards. *Out of the Crisis*, Cambridge, MA, MIT Center for Advanced Engineering Studies, 1986.

[8] Pasmore, William A. *Designing Effective Organizations: The Socio-Technical Systems Perspective*, New York, John Wiley & Sons, 1988.

and values. The role of the supervisor and the numbers of supervisors no longer made sense as the employees assumed more responsibility, and the information systems did not provide for employees gaining knowledge and control over their own work. The importance of the total culture and the underlying values was becoming more and more obvious.[9] We were increasingly addressing these issues but lacked a systematic methodology.

Forty years ago Eric Trist and others at the Tavistock Institute[10] in London began studying the environment of organizations and the interaction of the technical system of work and the social systems.

The foundation study of socio-technical design was conducted by Trist in British coal mines. He found that the traditional culture of the mines was one of small, self-selected, and highly interdependent groups of workers. When new technology was introduced into the mines, workers were assigned to single tasks controlled by external supervisors. The reactions of workers were negative and led to high absenteeism and low productivity. When workers were allowed to design their own organization, they duplicated their traditional cultural arrangements. Each person performed a number of different jobs as a member of a self-supervising work group. Productivity went up, and absenteeism went down.

There are two major precepts to socio-technical design theory. The first is *how well the social and technical systems are designed with respect to one another and with respect to the demands of the external environment determines how effective the organization will be.* The second is that *the organization is an open system.* This simple idea is that the organization like every living organism depends upon interaction with its environment. No organization is right or wrong, effective or ineffective, due to its own qualities alone. Rather, it is effective or ineffective due to how it meets the demands of the external environment. Because the external environment is constantly changing, the organization must remain an "open system," open to constant change and responsive to environmental needs. Its ability to adapt and change will ultimately determine its survival.

---

[9] Miller, Lawrence M. *American Spirit: Visions of A New Corporate Culture,* New York, Warner Books, 1984.

[10] Trist, E., Higgins, C., Murray, H., & Pollock, A. *Organizational Choice.* London, Tavistock Institute, 1963.

The idea of the organization as a system made up of interacting technical and social components is consistent with Dr. Deming's view of the system and the need to improve the process of work. The open-systems concept is another way of arriving at the conclusion that the organization must be "customer-focused" and must engage in continuous improvement to meet ever-changing customer needs.

Lean Production Systems

Perhaps the strongest force influencing change in corporations to-day is the competitive pressure and example of the Japanese. The Japanese transplants, particularly the NUMMI experience of a joint Toyota and General Motors plant in Fremont, California, and the Honda and Toyota experience in Marysville, Ohio, and Georgetown, Kentucky, have clearly demonstrated the superiority of a different system of production. The issue is not Japanese or American. The issue is not Roger Smith, Lee Iacocca, or the effect of the union. The issue is not "good guys" and "bad guys." The issue is the difference between one system of production versus another.

The evolution of production systems can be seen in three stages (which have been well- described in *The Machine That Changed The World*, the result of a five-year MIT comparative study of the global auto industry).[11] These stages are 1) craft production, 2) mass production, and 3) lean production. James P. Womack and Daniel T. Jones have recently describe their view on how to implement lean production systems in their Lean Thinking.[12]

The world is awash in buzz words. Buzz words are the toxic waste of management and organizational improvement. It will be most helpful if managers and employees understand the change process as one that is consistent with some historic inevitability. The nature of work and organizations is the reflection of larger trends such as education, information technology, and communications. The evolution of organization can be seen in three historic stages of development.

Stage I: Family Farm & Craft Shop: Most of our history on this planet saw work defined within small organizations: the family farm, and

---

[11] Womack, James P., Jones, Daniel T., & Roos, Daniel. *The Machine That Changed The World*, New York, Rawson Associates, 1990

[12] Womack, James P., Jones, Daniel T. *Lean Thinking: Banishing Waste and Create Wealth in Your Corporation*. New York, Simon & Schuster. 1996

the small craft shop. The family farm and craft shop were essentially the same type of organization: one did the outdoor work, the other the indoor work. But they had common characteristics. They were a small group of intimate individuals who were highly interdependent and psychologically close. They were a family. They shared roles and responsibilities, learning to perform all of the skills within the shop or on the farm, not restricted to single or simple tasks.

The craft shops did not make their product unless they received an order from a customer. They could not afford to warehouse furniture or instruments. They were "custom made," thus assuring a close relationship with the customer. Each unit of a product, each piece of furniture, musical instrument, or wagon was unique and had to have its parts fit together individually. This craftsmanship required high skill and patience and was time-consuming. This was the standard system of production before the automobile.

The organization of the family farm and small craft shop was both a technical work system and a social system. Both the technical and social aspects must be analyzed to understand the impact on the individual and the quality of the product.

The advantage of this system was not only its flexibility but its ability to provide a psychologically nurturing environment. Although most Americans have never set foot on a family farm, they still talk of the family farm with a romantic fondness. This fondness is not because of its efficiency but because of its ability to meet the needs of its members. It was a far more effective human system than a production system.

Stage II: Mass Production - Henry Ford's Factory: The industrial revolution, characterized by the development of large, impersonal, efficient systems of mass production, changed the nature of work and management forever. This change was no mere fad. Ford's factory was the archetype of the mass production organization.

There were two major factors in Ford's success. The first was achieving the inter-changeability of parts. Before mass production each part, each gear, piston, or tie rod had to be individually fitted. Skilled fitters were the most skilled and highest paid workers in assembly plants before mass production. Ford and his associates developed production techniques that relied on prehardened metals and superior casting techniques, and they religiously insisted on common measurement methods to assure inter-changeable parts. The second key to Ford's success was the moving assembly line that reduced the motion of workers, simplified their work, and resulted in the inter-changeability of the workforce.

Henry Ford's factory employed thousands of new immigrants who reportedly spoke as many as fifty different languages. Workers working next to each other often could not communicate. Job simplification and control by supervision were essential to the process.

In the inefficient craft shop the workers would make decisions to improve their own work. On the assembly line the workers were separated from the improvement process. Improvement was turned over to specialists, industrial engineers, who studied and defined work methods. Industrial engineers became specialized, some in die change, casting, and assembly. A hierarchy of engineers developed with their own organizations. Accounting, marketing, design, and others followed the model, each developing his own language, increasingly complex and increasingly separate from the others. Walls were being built. The walls were not only between departments but between methods of thought, communication, and understanding. These are the walls that would eventually lead to bureaucracy and inefficiency.

The emergence of Ford's factory was paralleled by the development of scientific management championed by Frederick Taylor. Taylor is most often the subject derisive comments today, however, it must be acknowledged that Taylor's methods and thought process brought a mental discipline, a scientific rigor, to the production process that had previously been absent. Taylor and his followers taught managers to study their data, to gather data on the productivity of the system and to analyze the efficiency of the system in a rigorous manner. This was essential to the improvement in productivity that increased the wealth of the nation and the world. This emphasis on "the facts" is still very evident in the best practices of lean production systems and other world class organizations. Taylor's view of the worker however, was entirely demeaning. He viewed the worker as a tool of the production process and saw no place for the employee to make decisions are participate in responsibility for improvement. Taylor was no psychologist. He was pure engineer. He did not understand the needs for participation, shared responsibility, and dignity. Nor did he respect their intelligence.

It is critical to understand the change in the psychology of work. Workers were no longer awarded the honor of the craftsman. Self-esteem and self-respect were denied to the worker who was told to "do your own work." Thinking and improvement had become a separate profession, requiring degrees and licenses to practice. The intimacy of the family group, a requirement of our species, was no longer available in the work place. It was soon replaced by another form of organization, a counter force to the large and intimidating corporation. Unions were a natural response the loss of power and self-esteem imposed the mass production organization. In this counter organization individuals would again feel that they were "brothers" and "sisters."

Stage III: The Lean Organization: In my view the lean organization or the total quality organization has evolved from all of the schools of thought we have already discussed. However, the organization that brought this thinking together and added its practical and most successful development was again in the auto industry, this time in Japan.

The third stage of production began in post World War II Japan, and Eiji Toyoda and Taiichi Ohno must be credited with its development. Contrary to the belief of many in the quality profession, it is this different system of production and organization that is the primary determinant of quality, not statistical methods, despite their obvious value.

In 1949, Toyota's sales collapsed, and they were forced to lay off large numbers of workers. This collapse followed a lengthy and bitter strike by their union. By 1950, Toyota had produced a total of only 2,685 cars, compared to one Ford plant that produced more than 7,000 each day. Eiji Toyoda made many trips to Ford's River Rouge plant in Dearborn to study the most efficient production system in the world. He concluded that the Ford system could not succeed in Japan.

The environment in Japan was different. First, the market was small and required a wide variety of different types of vehicles. Long production runs of identical cars and parts were not possible. Second, the workforce and their unions would no longer accept being treated as insignificant interchangeable parts. Labor laws introduced by the American occupational forces had so strengthened the unions that they represented everyone, eliminating the distinction between white and blue collar workers. They had also negotiated a share of the profits. Third, capital was scarce, making heavy expenditures for the latest technology impossible.

The development of "lean production" methods by Toyoda's production chief, Taiichi Ohno, was a response to this environment. It began with the stamping of body parts.

In the craft shop, body panels were hammered by hand into shape. The metal sheet was laid over a die and gradually shaped by hammering the metal. Aston-Martin and Morgan still use this method. Contrary to myth, this step does not produce a superior product to mass production methods; it is simply more expensive. In Ford's factory the production of body parts was based on large quantities of identical metal sheets being placed in a die and stamped into shape. The quantities of identical parts required in Ford's factories allowed for die presses to be dedicated to single parts. There were die change engineers who supervised the die change process. Changing a die usually required one or two days of machine downtime. Ohno concluded that this second method was impossible due to the quantities required for efficient operation. Toyota could not afford dedicated die presses. If they used this method to change dies, the stamping presses would be inoperative half of the time. Ohno had to develop a system whereby dies could be changed every couple of hours. This meant that the die change process had to be reduced from days to minutes.[13]

Ohno developed a system of rollers that allowed dies to be quickly moved in and out of place by the workers themselves. He concluded after experimentation that the requirement of specialists slowed the process down. It could be accomplished quickly only if the workers working as a team had the knowledge and skills to perform the task themselves. In order to do this they not only had to have the necessary skills; they had to have knowledge of the larger production process to know when to change dies. They had to accept full responsibility for their own work.

In accomplishing this quick die change process, Taiichi Ohno had established a pattern that would be replicated throughout the factory. Small groups of workers would be treated as full partners in the process, responsible for their own work, able to improve and modify their process, and having knowledge of the previous and next stages of production (their internal customers and suppliers) so that they would understand the requirements and effect of their work. Ohno found that these work groups, given the necessary information, worked to continuously improve their work process.

On the assembly line Ohno formed workers into teams with a working team leader rather than a foreman. Teams were given a set of assembly steps and told to work together to devise the best possible ways to accomplish the assembly. The team leader would participate in

---

[13] Ohno, Taiichi & Mito, Setsuo. *Just-In-Time For Today and Tomorrow*. Cambridge, MA, Productivity Press, 1986.

the work, stepping in to help where needed. These teams soon accepted responsibility for housekeeping, small machine repair, maintenance, and checking their own quality. The teams would meet periodically to find ways to continuously improve (**Kaizen**) their process.

The total system in the Toyota plants became distinctly different than in American auto plants. Lots were small, and quick change-to-order was a priority. They achieved the combination of efficiency and small production runs which American producers assumed to be contradictory. This was accomplished only by completely redefining the system of work and worker responsibility. It was a whole new system.

Ohno's system had implications for all areas of the business and organization. Engineering and design teams now functioned in a fast-cycle process. The need for quick response, quick change, and just-in-time was extended to supplier relations. These processes produced a different type of organization than was developing in Detroit. Toyota required few layers of management with less distinction in function, pay, and status between workers and managers while Detroit was increasing layers and distinctions.

Business Process Reengineering

Business process reengineering has been one of the hottest buzz words in management this decade. There are two distinct differences between whole system management and the practice of reengineering. First, whole system management focuses on building an organizational capability to meet future customer needs and build business, rather than simply cutting costs or improving efficiency. Second, it focuses on people as much as technical work process, creating a competitive culture.

Michael Hammer and James Champy[14] define reengineering as "starting over." It means abandoning long-established procedures and looking afresh at the work required to create a company's product or service and deliver value to the customer. It means asking the question, "If I were recreating this company today given what I know and given current technology, what would it look like?" Reengineering a company means tossing aside old systems and starting over.

---

[14] Hammer, Michael & Champy, James. *Reeingineering The Corporation: A Manifesto For Business Revolution*. New York, N.Y., Harper Business, 1993.

This definition is very close to whole system management or organizational redesign. Both study the needs of customers to define the requirements for work processes. Both map out the flow of processes to identify waste and combine functions or activities. Both start with a clean sheet of paper. Both can produce dramatic change. Only one is based on an appreciation of the whole system.

During the past several years we have consulted in a number of organizations at the same time or immediately after another consultant worked with the organization on reengineering business processes. The result and emphasis were very clear. The focus was on cost improvement and the elimination of work. This is not a criticism. I have no doubt that this was a step forward and a necessary improvement. What was not done, however, was to create a new social system or a new way of working together that would lead to future business gains. There was no effort to create the skills and the competencies that would be necessary for future competition.

Reengineering is neo-Taylorism. Reengineering breaks the process down into its component parts, assumes that there is a linear relationship of one step leading to the next, as on an automotive assembly line, with each step measurable in time and cost. Sometimes this is true. However, as we will discuss in Chapter Six, more than half of the work done in the United States and other advanced economies is non-production and non-linear. The mental model of reengineering and Frederick Taylor fails to capture the complexity of knowledge based work systems. It is reported that seventy percent of reengineering projects have failed to improve business performance. One explanation for this is that the paradigm upon which reengineering is based does not address the essential value-adding work of so many of our companies today.

Peter Drucker explained it well: "The basic economic resource - 'means of production,' to use the economist's term - is no longer capital, nor natural resources (the economist's *land*), nor labor. It is and will be knowledge. The central wealth creating activities will be neither the allocation of capital to productive uses, nor labor - the two poles of nineteenth and twentieth century economic theory, whether classical, Marxist, Keynesian, or neo-classical. Value is now created by 'productivity' and 'innovation,' both applications of knowledge to work. The leading social groups of the knowledge society will be 'knowledge-workers' - knowledge executives who know how to allocate knowledge to productive use; knowledge professionals; knowledge employees. Practically all these knowledge people will be employed in organizations. Yet unlike the employees under Capitalism, they will own both the 'means of production' and the 'tools of production' - the former through their pension funds, which are rapidly emerging in all developed countries as the only real owners; the latter because knowledge workers own their knowledge and can take it with them wherever they go. The economic challenge of the post capitalist society will therefore be the productivity of knowledge work and the knowledge worker."[15]

In the knowledge work culture the importance of human capital, the intelligence of the enterprise, the captured corporate knowledge is the greatest asset of the corporation. We all remember the old General Electric commercials that proclaimed "progress through people" and all of the slogans proclaiming that people are our most important asset. This is not genuinely true. Workers own the knowledge. The company cannot lock it up, rarely can it be copyrighted, and there are virtually no secrets in the age of the Internet. For this reason, a reengineering model based on the linear assumptions of production work are doomed to failure. Today relationship are a critical ingredient in competitive success. Trust may become more important than speed in the near future.

The business environment is increasingly one in which long term customer and supplier relationships are essential and built on trust. The merchant trading in the bazaar of the Middle East was skilled at tricking the customer into paying more than an item was worth. The negotiation between customer and supplier was a game played with subtle cultural rules that allowed for a level of dishonesty by both parties. In today's environment "guaranteed customer satisfaction" is offered by Wal-Mart and Sears and you can return the item, no questions asked. An Internet search will turn up the medical success rate of hospitals, pharmaceuticals, vitamins, the performance of cars, customer satisfaction of hotels and airlines. Companies focus on creating "brand-equity" the value inherent in a name, a name which can be trusted to represent value. The Toyota Production System model of manufacturing is built on the creation of long term and intricately close relationships through the supply chain. In this world class manufacturing model suppliers invest huge sums to build manufacturing plants next to their customer's plant to provide just-in-time flow of incoming materials. All of these realities of today's business environment require long term relationships built on trust.

---

[15] Drucker, Peter. *Post-Capitalist Society.* New York, Harper Business, 1993. P. 8.

A recent and popular book by Francis Fukuyama[16] presents a well thought out argument that *"one of the most important lessons we can learn from an examination of economic life is that a nation's well-being, as well as its ability to compete, is conditioned by a single, pervasive cultural characteristic: the level of trust inherent in the society."*

This analysis of high trust society as a foundation of wealth presents a clear warning to cultures such as the United States in which the decline of sociability, the loss of trust, is rapid and visible. It is also a warning to the corporation and managers who still believe they can manage through intimidation and a focus only on the financial numbers of the business. The creation of trust within and between corporations and their customers is a strategic requirement. This demands a reengineering of the whole system and clear alignment between the business, work and human systems of the organization.

Complex Systems Theory

Chaos theory may be one step beyond useful to most managers. However, for those struggling with the transformation of their organizations, understanding complex systems may be the key to creating order from apparent chaos. Complexity matters. It defines the difference between successfully managing a McDonald's restaurant and a pharmaceutical research lab and why the misapplication of management techniques, such as reengineering and performance measurement, can stifle the productivity of knowledge work.

In the organization that adds value through knowledge and creativity rather than the visible order of "A" followed by "B" leading to "C" the linear reengineering analysis of work may be of little use. In knowledge work there may be one thousand "A's" occurring in parallel and all communicating instantly with one another, while "B's" and "C's" listen in a dozen countries and provide feedback from diverse perspectives. That confusing example is a simple case. From this apparently chaotic virtual beehive of work may come the creative output that is the new software, computer, or marketing plan and any attempt to frame it in Taylor's linear view would destroy its genius. This is the knowledge-work organization. How do you design organization, systems, or man-

---

[16] Fukuyama, Francis: *Trust: The Social Virtues & The Creation of Prosperity*, New York, The Free Press, 1995.

agement practices to support this complexity? Some of the answers may be found in the study of complex systems found in other sciences.

Much scientific research has been based on the reductionist approach found in physics, chemistry and behavioral psychology in which the scientist studies the relationships between variables by controlling the number of variables to simplify the environment hoping to discover the direct relationship, one variable to another. The Skinner box, in which a pigeon was isolated, the environment controlled and discrete behavior measured and manipulated by schedules of reinforcement is an example of this method. Through this process much useful knowledge was discovered. However, the real environment is very different. The study of medicine and the cause of disease in the human body is much more complicated. The human body and its interaction with the environment represent one complex system interacting with another complex system.

We have all heard someone report that they didn't believe smoking caused cancer because they knew someone ninety years old who had been smoking for seventy years and was as healthy as an ox. It's true. Everyone who smokes does not contract cancer. Everybody is unique and everybody is simultaneously interacting with hundreds of other agents in the air, food, the community, and at home. We all know that two chemicals may be poured together with no reaction. Mixed with a third, they may explode. It is the interaction of variables, often hundreds at a time, that define a complex system. The causes of cancer may not be a one-to-one relationship of variables. It may the result of multiple variables interacting in the right sequence at the right time. It is a complex relationship. For this reason the process defies description in the straight line, linear fashion, of process mapping.

The free economy is a complex system. When Russians, schooled in the tradition and culture of control and bureaucratic decision making dominant in the old Soviet Union, came to the United States they would ask what seemed like perfectly rationale questions. "Who decides who can start a company?" And the answer, of course, is anyone! Unbelievable to the controlling Russian mind. "Well, then, who decides who gets capital and how much capital?" Well, sort of anyone. Whoever wants to put in capital may and it sort of depends on how much noise the entrepreneur makes. It's sort of a free for all. Again, it was hard for the Russian mind to comprehend that decisions so important could be so chaotic. How could these Americans be good at business when they don't even seem to know how these decisions are made? Perhaps they are trying to deceive us! Its easy to image the skepticism on the part of Russian bureaucrats.

We are so conditioned to the workings of our free economy that we take the near chaos, the complexity of the process, for granted. There is order in a complex system. However, it is a very different kind of order than in Ford's factory or in a McDonald's restaurant. It is an order of probabilities. An order of principles, of attractions, of tendencies, rather than of control. There is a logic and order to how companies acquire capital. But it is not controlled order. It is the law of free market capital flow with revenue growth and return on investment acting as "strange attractors", like magnets pulling money toward the company. This is the type of order found in complex systems.

One of the founders of the science of complexity was Alan Turing who was an unsung hero of World War II. He was the supreme code breaker who unraveled the mystery of messages sent by the German navel Enigma machines.[17] The British and U.S. governments still prevent open discussion of the methods he used although some have called his contribution the single most important contribution to Allied victory in Europe. Turing's ambition was to construct the artificial brain, the computer that could think. Turing was convinced of the importance of learning and intelligence and spent much of his time studying the structure of brain cells and how they act together during learning. This work was the foundation of the digital revolution and it was built on the study of complex systems in nature.

As knowledge work expands, as work increasingly becomes shared across companies and nations, as place becomes less important and connections and interaction become more important, as the Internet becomes the factory, we are working in a complex system. Whole system thinking is essential to the management of these systems. A focus on only one part of the system minimizes the opportunity to shape the behavior of the complex system. Managers must become scientists of the new science of complexity and whole systems.

---

[17] Conveney, Peter and Highfield, Roger. *Frontiers of Complexity: The Search for Order in a Chaotic World*, New York, Facett Columbine, 1995.

Assistance

Our Mission

The mission of Miller/Howard Consulting Group is to enhance the quality of work and worklife for our clients and our society; to contribute to the material, intellectual, and spiritual wealth of our clients; to advance the skills and knowledge of our field; and to contribute to the total well being of our associates. We are dedicated to the principles of democracy, free expression, and enhancement of self-esteem of all through self-management and teamwork.

Consulting

For over two decades, Miller/Howard Consulting Group has been a leader in organizational change. Our extensive experience has taught us that training works well to initiate change, but lasting improvement requires comprehensive follow-up. The experienced professionals at Miller/Howard Consulting Group are available to assist you toward your pursuit of becoming a high performance organization.

We work at every level of the organization, from the chief executive to the entry level, and have implemented our methodologies in a variety of industries, ranging from Fortune 1000 companies to small businesses.

Our clients have included the following companies:

Air Canada
Alabama Power Company
Alcan Cable
Allina Health Systems
Amoco Production Company
Augusta Newsprint Company
Avery Dennison
Bell Canada
The Bradford Exchange
Chick-fil-A
Clark-Schwebel
Collins & Aikman Products Company
Corning
Dad's Products Company
Delmarva Power & Light Company
Dial Corporation
Dun's Marketing Services

Murray Ohio Manufacturing
NationsBank
Northern States Power
Olin Ordnance
Petroleum Development Oman
Pharmacia & Upjohn
Plymouth Tube Company
Printpack
QuikTrip
Sara Lee Corporation
Scott Paper Company
Shell Canada
Shell Chemical Company
Shell Oil Company
Southwestern Bell
Springs Industries
Star Paper Tube

Eastman Kodak
Engelhard Corporation
Exxon U.S.A.
Georgetown Steel Corporation
Harris Corporation
Landmark Communications
McDonald's Corporation
Merck
Metropolitan Life Insurance Company
Moody's Investor Services

Star Tribune
SunTrust Banks
Tennessee Eastman Company
Texaco Refining & Marketing
Texaco U.S.A.
United Technologies
Varig Airlines
Wellman
Xerox Corporation

Change Management Seminars and Products

All seminars are offered as public courses as well as customized, on-site programs. Some programs and products are available in Spanish and French.

For additional information call (404) 255-6523
http://www.millerhoward.com

Seminars:
Consultant Training School
Introduction to Change Management

This seminar teaches the fundamentals of good consulting, including how to: help your client articulate a positive vision of your organization's future; develop an implementation plan to accomplish this vision; manage the dynamics of individual and organizational change; and determine organizational readiness. You will also learn the interpersonal skills critical to becoming an effective consultant, including active listening, assertiveness, persuasion, negotiating, and behavioral contracting. Different models for organizational interventions will be discussed, including strategy planning, Whole System Architecture, and team-based organizations.

Leading Change Management

This one-day overview will provide you with an understanding of whole system methodology to create the future capabilities, organization, systems, and processes that will lead to your competitive success. Also available as a customized, on-site program is a three-day Whole System Architecture seminar that will facilitate a greater understanding of how to design and implement whole system change in your organization.

Organization Design School
A Whole System Approach

This four-day seminar offers an in-depth look at how to effectively create and implement organizational change from a whole systems viewpoint. As organizations move through various stages of improvement, internal consultants need increased knowledge and understanding of whole systems design to create a well-aligned organization. This course is designed to provide training, skills, practice, and a strong foundation for those who need advanced knowledge and skills regarding Whole System Architecture, redesign, reengineering, and large-scale change. This is a great opportunity to learn from others who are creating dynamic organizations.

Creating a Team-based Organization

This seminar introduces participants to the essential skills needed for establishing a dynamic organization. As a participant, you will learn how to develop an organizational culture based on the principles and characteristics of a high performance organization; implement natural work teams for continuous improvements in quality, productivity, cycle times, and costs; design an implementation plan for organization change; plan and manage team meetings and group interaction to have a significant impact on business results; and establish measurement criteria and feedback systems for continuous improvement.

Team Consultant Training School

During this course participants will focus on two avenues of interventions: coaching team meetings and teaching team effectiveness skills. Participants will learn how to develop an implementation plan for creating a team-based organization, including how to identify and successfully complete critical milestones and measures. Participants will also receive instruction in how to train the Team Management modules and use the Trainer's Toolkit. Through role plays, class presentations, and group feedback participants will sharpen the skills essential to effective team consulting.

Advanced Team Consultant Training School

This course is structured for internal consultants who have experience implementing a team-based organization. We will delve into the specific challenges of implementing teams throughout your organization and cover topics such as team assessments, project management, new roles for managers and leaders, aligning teams with business strategy, and group dynamics and group process.

Customized Advanced Team Training

Most of the topics featured in *The Advanced Team Guide* can be delivered as customized training programs for your organization.

Workbooks:

Change Management
Creating the Dynamic Organization Through Whole System Architecture

Whole system design and implementation is clearly explained in the 400+ page *Change Management* workbook. The change management process described in the book is based on the authors' years of experience and knowledge on how best to transform an organization and its culture to a high performance system. Specific chapter topics that will guide you through this transformation include an overview of the organization as a dynamic system, principles of Whole System Architecture, how to prepare for change, the roles and responsibilities of leading a change effort, understanding and creating the business system strategy and scorecard, writing the design charter, designing the work and human systems, aligning and implementing the new architecture, and how to use conference methodology for high involvement design. Insightful case studies are located throughout the book along with exercises, action steps, and assessment tools.

The Internal Consultant's Guide
Tools and Techniques to Create and Sustain a High Performance Organization

This 185+ page workbook provides coaches, facilitators, and internal consultants with essential coaching skills to guide them through managing change and implementation. Topics covered include how to manage change and an organizational change model; creating, monitoring, and managing the implementation process; the role of the internal consultant; interpersonal skills critical to effective internal consultants; and internal consultant tips.

Team Management
Creating Systems and Skills for a Team-based Organization

The 330+ page *Team Management* workbook provides both team leaders and members with the necessary skills to create and sustain a high-performance organization. Topics include establishing teams, the changing role of leadership, the organizational systems required to support teams, defining customer requirements, developing scorecards, having effective meetings, decision-making, assessments, and problem-solving.

Team Management
A Guide for Trainers

The easy-to-follow 130+ page *Team Management* trainer's guide provides the team trainer with invaluable training tips for each step in the Team Management process. Playful illustrations highlight key training topics, while exercises, action items, troubleshooting, and helpful hints offer you practical advice and guidance on creating, implementing, and maintaining teams as a part of your day-to-day business operations.

Team Management
Team Trainer's Toolkit

The *Team Management* Team Trainer's Toolkit accompanies Miller/Howard Consulting Group's *Team Management* workbook and seminar series. The toolkit consists of nearly 100 full-color overheads and *Team Management: A Guide for Trainers*. Each overhead illustrates a key learning point in the *Team Management* workbook, covering all of the skills needed by teams to define their customers and requirements, create a scorecard, participate in problem solving, and continuously improve their processes.

The Advanced Team Guide
Tools, Techniques, and Tips for Experienced Teams

Finally, a guidebook that addresses key issues teams face as they mature. The 400+ page book provides useful, practical suggestions for team leaders, members, and coaches as they internalize the principles of a team-based organization. With over a hundred years of combined experience, the authors share their knowledge, expertise, and experience about how to make teams successful in your organization. Chapters in the book include exercises, case studies, and examples about issues every team faces in its development, such as technology and teams; alternate compensation and teams; aligning teams with business strategy; team structure; team and individual feedback; new roles for managers and leaders; advanced performance analysis; advanced problem solving and decision-making; managing diversity and differences; group process and group dynamics; and frequently occurring problems and how to solve them.

Books

AMERICAN SPIRIT: Visions of a New Corporate Culture
By Lawrence M. Miller

This remarkable book plots a course for the future of American management as Mr. Miller redefines corporate culture and the relationship between managers and workers. He explains by means of eight revolutionary principles the most important elements of competitive advantage. This book provides a specific plan of action for every executive and for every company on the way to the top. Available in hardback and paperback.

BARBARIANS TO BUREAUCRATS: Corporate Life Cycle Strategies
By Lawrence M. Miller

This book presents a brilliant new solution to an old business problem: how to halt a company's descent into stifling bureaucracy. Mr. Miller argues that corporations, like civilizations, have a natural life cycle and that by identifying the stage your company is in, and the leaders associated with it, you can avert decline and continue to thrive. Available in hardback or paperback.

BEYOND CORPORATE TRANSFORMATION:
A Whole Systems Approach to Creating and Sustaining High Performance
By Christopher W. Head

Unlike most books written by a consultant that express only one perspective, *Beyond Corporate Transformation* incorporates the views, insights, and change methodologies from several of the finest management consulting firms and a number of leading-edge companies. The author's research for *Beyond Corporate Transformation* indicated that the companies most successful in their change efforts take a holistic approach to change as opposed to jumping from one change program to another. The book provides a methodology for educating, preparing, and leading employees through the many stages necessary to transform the organization into one that is capable of creating and sustaining a lasting competitive advantage.